Historical Background

'There is in the handling of these Transatlantic ships a nucleus of trouble for the Navy of Great Britain.'

Admiral Lord Nelson on sighting American merchant ships from 1801 to 1803

Profit from international trade is the lifeblood of any nation. Of all the nations, Great Britain well understood the strategic importance of trade and built a large and effective navy to protect it and disrupt the trade of any opposing nation. The Royal Navy employed well-practised tactics such as the long-term blockade of enemy harbours and fleet actions that effectively destroyed any navy that would otherwise disrupt British shipping. The British had perfected these techniques to such a degree that they were used in the Second World War to prevent German commerce raiders such as the *Admiral Graf Spee* and *Bismarck* from seriously threatening merchant convoys.

When thirteen of Britain's North American colonies declared their independence, American merchant trade immediately lost the protection of the Royal Navy. Although several European nations recognised the United States as a new country – primarily because it furthered their opposition to British hegemony since the Seven Years' War, little tangible support was provided to the new country. The United States had no navy to protect her shipping and being saddled with enormous war debts to France and several other European countries for their support in the war for independence it could ill afford to build one. Moreover, Europe, and in particular Great Britain, was also America's greatest market for her vast natural resources, which meant that the bulk of America's merchant fleet was sailing in European waters with no protection, putting the country's primary source of income – customs and excise revenue – at grave peril. The shifting alliances amongst European nations also meant that nations friendly to the United States might instantly become an enemy that stopped and seized its shipping. There was little the American government could do besides lodging diplomatic protests or try to negotiate a treaty, but the United States had no means to enforce any treaty signed. Besides, most American politicians favoured landward expansion to diversify the American economy and coveted the annexation of Upper and Lower Canada (the present-day provinces of Ontario and Québec, respectively), Britain's loyal North American colonies.

THE BARBARY STATES

Managing shifting European alliances was just one issue, but the most immediate problem was the North African regencies of Morocco, Algiers, Tunis, and Tripoli collectively known as the Barbary States. Morocco had its own ruler but the others were nominally under the suzerainty of the Ottoman Turks, although a *Bey* (governor) ruled each regency largely independently. The region soon developed into a centre for *corsairs* (privateers) that preyed on international trade along Africa's Mediterranean and Atlantic coasts. Any nation's shipping was considered fair game unless protected by a treaty with a Bey not to molest their ships, granted in exchange for annual tributes of *specie* (money in the form of coins, not notes) and gifts. Ships of countries with no agreement were seized and their crews were held for ransom as leverage for annual tribute; and if no agreement could be reached, were sold into slavery. The ships themselves were often taken into the Beys' naval forces and over time they grew to be large and powerful, their ships ranging from large cannon-armed feluccas to sloops and brigs of western design. In 1785 the Algerian corsairs began to seize American merchant vessels, but for the United States it was simpler to pay annual tribute. By 1800 the United States had paid Tripoli alone over two million dollars ($48.6 million in 2024 dollars).

In 1794 the decision to create a navy was finally taken, but the role of this new US Navy was a delicate balancing act: on the one hand, it was intended to check the Barbary states, but it should not compromise American neutrality in order to allow trade with as many nations as possible, and it was not to be large enough to provoke a new war with Britain. These considerations were complicated by two treaties with Royalist France signed in 1778. The first was the mutual defence pact known as the 'Treaty of Alliance' whereby the United States agreed to protect the French West Indies in return for French support in the

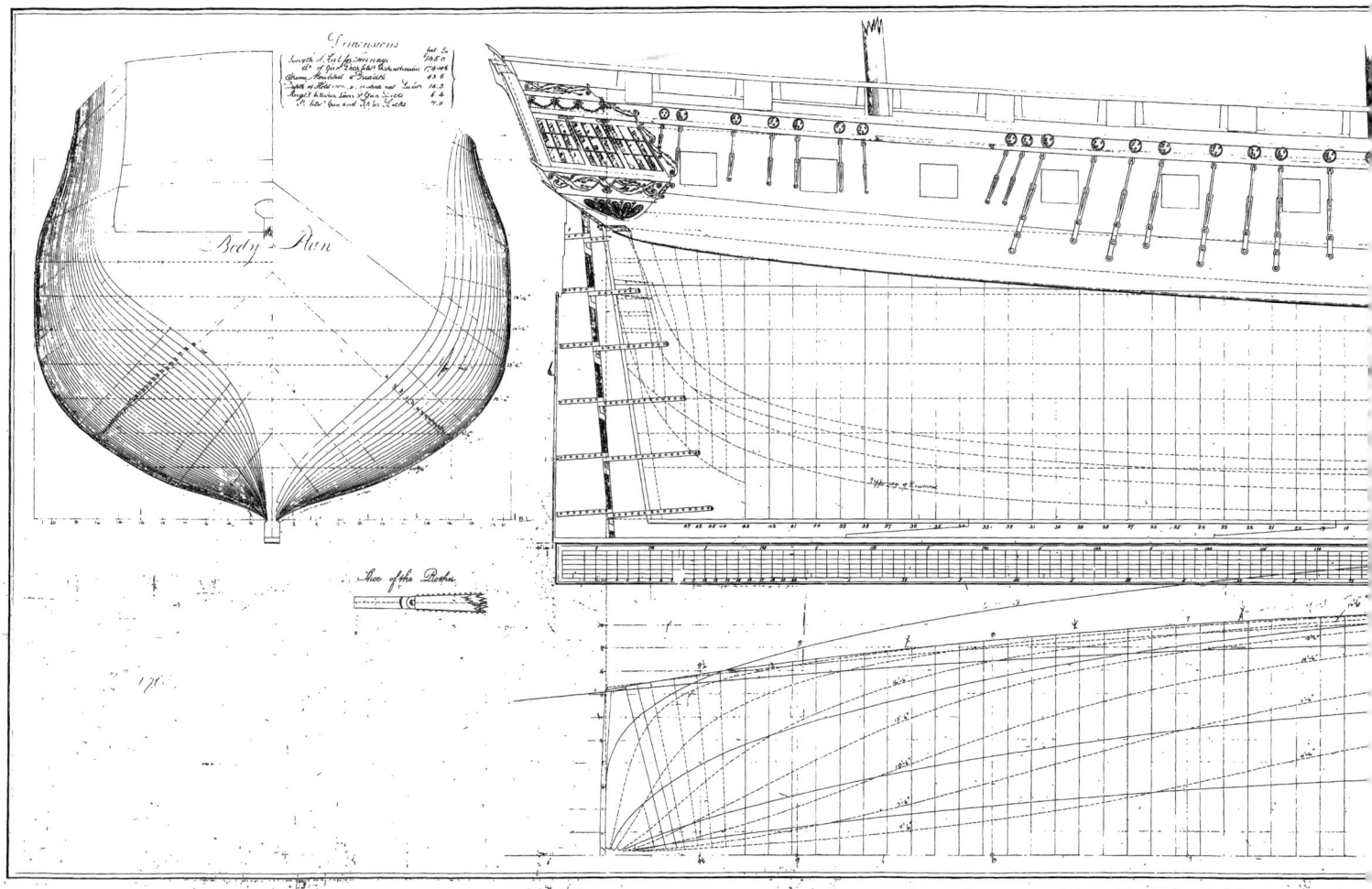

war for independence. The treaty also forbade either nation from making a separate peace with Great Britain. The second was the 'Treaty of Amity and Commerce' that established mutual trade and navigation rights between France and the United States. As such, any American navy that would sail alongside the French would likely provoke a war with Britain – and also with Spain, which was at war with France at the time. Moreover, in any war the loyalist colonies on America's northern border would pose a serious risk, as Britain could easily transport armies to the Canadas and send them into the United States.

The reticence ended with a petition from Baltimore merchants demanding naval protection for their ships owing to the ruinous insurance rates charged against their vessels. President Washington signed 'An Act to Provide a Naval Armament' on 27 March 1794 that authorised the construction of six 44-gun frigates to be named the *United States*, *Constellation*, *Congress*, *Chesapeake*, *President*, and *Constitution*. However, President Washington was ever cognizant of costs and included a clause that would halt construction of the ships if peace terms were agreed with Algiers. As a further hedge against provoking a war with European powers, Washington signed the 'Neutrality Act' of 1794 that prohibited American citizens from enlisting or accepting commissions in foreign military forces, fitting out foreign privateers and warships, or participating in *filibuster expeditions* (an unauthorised military expedition into a foreign country or territory to foster or support a political revolution). Additionally, he made a Presidential Executive Order that forbade American merchant ships from arming themselves.

DESIGN AND CONSTRUCTION

In a letter dated 6 January 1793, the shipbuilder Joshua Humphreys who had built ships for the colonial navy during the American revolutionary war, discussed the characteristics he proposed for the ships of the new navy:

> … our navy must for a considerable time be inferior in numbers, we are to consider what size ships will be most formidable and be an over-match for those of an enemy; such Frigates as in blowing weather would be an over-match for double deck ships, and in light winds to evade coming to action, or double deck ships as would be an over-match for common double deck ships and in blowing weather superior to ships of three decks, or in calm weather or light winds to outsail them. Ships built on these principles will render those of an enemy in a degree useless, or require

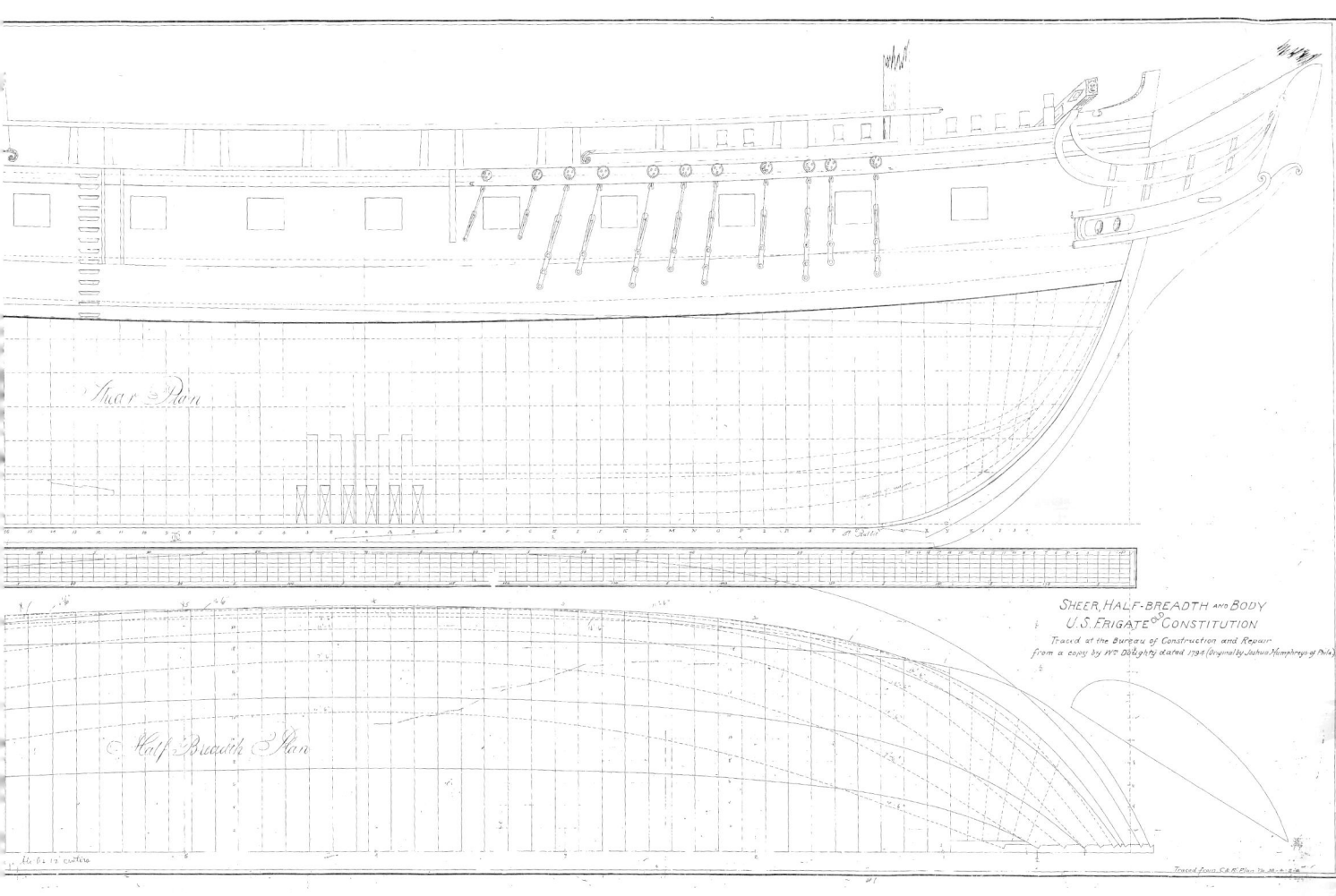

Humphreys' ideas for the ships of the new US Navy materialised in his draughts. *Constitution*'s sheer, half-breadth and body plan traced from William Doughty's copy of Humphreys' original draught dated 1794. *(Naval History & Heritage Command Detachment Boston)*

a greater number before they dare attack our ship. Frigates, I suppose, will be the first object and none ought to be built less than 150 feet keel to carry 28 32-pounders or 30 24-pounders on the gun deck and 12-pounders on the quarterdeck. These ships should have scantlings equal to 74's ... they should be built of best materials that could possibly be procured ... (Full transcript of the letter held at the Historical Society of Pennsylvania).

Humphreys created a half model to illustrate his ideas. The ships were not those that would stand in the line of battle but instead would cruise independently, much like contemporary British Fifth Rate vessels. Fifth Rates in the Royal Navy were the standard frigates, whose role was scouting and trade protection; their main battery from the 1780s consisted of twenty-six or twenty-eight 18-pounders, with smaller 9- or 6-pounder guns on the quarterdeck and forecastle. Burthen (a calculation of tonnage) ranged from 800 to 1150 tons, with crews of 215 to 294 men. However, the new American ships would have a much longer hull of around 175ft making them 20ft longer than any Fifth Rate, with an extreme *beam* (width) that was 3ft greater than standard British ships, and at least 13ft longer and one-foot greater than the largest contemporary French frigates of similar guns. Uniquely, Humphreys' design incorporated a flush 'spar deck' connecting the forecastle and quarterdeck to create a continuous deck capable of supporting additional guns along its entire length.

Humphreys also sought to create a hull that was thicker than British or French naval vessels. He accomplished this by reducing the space between the frames that made up the hull, a dimension known as the 'room and space'. This provision ensured an optimal spacing between the frames for ventilation to prevent damp and rot. Room and space is measured as the distance between a frame's face edge to the equivalent face edge of the next frame. The room and space on a British 44-gun ship was about 28.5 inches, and depending on the moulded dimension of the frame, the actual space between two frames was 4 to 6 inches apart. In Humphreys' design, the space between two frames was reduced to about two inches throughout the hull and the closely spaced frames along with the spar deck allowed his ship to carry much larger guns. However, a consequence of the additional weight of the hull frames is to cause the hull to sag at both ends – a phenomenon called 'hogging'. In contemporary ship construction, the frames were bolted to the ship's keel and the hull stiffened by the planking on the outside of the frames (composing the outer hull planking)

This drawing of *Congress*' sail plan in 1799 (drawn by Charles Ware in 1818) provides an example of how Humphreys' design appeared at sea. *Congress* and *Constellation* were built to a reduced version of the Humphreys draught for *Constitution*, but *Chesapeake* was smaller still due to alterations to the design made by the shipwright Josiah Fox before she was built. Note the postwar spencers – the gaff-headed fore-and-aft sails abaft the masts – that were also carried by *Constitution*. (National Archives and Records Administration – NARA)

and on the inside of the frames (called ceiling planks), and stout belt of thick timbers called the *wale* (or *bend*). These planks alone were insufficient to prevent hogging, which was made worse by the weight of guns and in Humphreys' design, the weight of additional frames and guns to be carried.

Ship designers experimented with different types of stiffeners called *riders*, such as a series of timbers or metal plates across the inside of the hull planking. Humphreys elected to fit six pairs of diagonal riders that rose from the sides of the *keelson* (a reinforcing timber that is fitted on top of the keel that runs the length of the hull) joined to the opposite ends of the berth deck (in a frigate the unarmed deck that houses the crew's accommodation and hammocks). The berth deck beams were also connected to the gun deck by three lines of stanchions running the length of the ship, along with a pair of thick deck planks on both sides of the main hatch that ran the length of both decks. Humphreys' design was an attempt to create an integrated system of timber that evenly distributed the weight of the gun deck and its armament to the berth deck and ultimately via the diagonals to the centre of the keel and reduce the forces acting on ends of the ship that cause hogging. The system was good in theory but not practice. A 1970s US Navy study of the ship, undertaken as part of the restoration of the ship for the 1976 bicentennial celebrations, examined the effectiveness of Humphreys' diagonal riders:

> ... the riders were found to have little effect on the bending response of the *Constitution*. Deformation of pinned connections contributes to the progression of hog in a wooden ship. This deformation is due to bearing stresses, pin deformation and pin corrosion. The riders may contribute to reducing the hogging rate of the *Constitution*, particularly in the short term, by virtue of the tightly fastened joints between the riders and the hull. The analytical and experimental evaluations of the proposed riders, however, did not account for these effects. (pp20–21).

Indeed, when the ship was launched the hull took on a pronounced hog that was never corrected during her service life.

BUILDING *CONSTITUTION*

There remains some controversy over the credit for *Constitution*'s final hull lines. Although Joshua Humphreys produced the original draught, a new immigrant to the United States, Josiah Fox, may have altered that draught. Fox was a skilled naval architect who had been apprenticed for about three and a half years as a shipwright in England at the Royal Dockyards at Plymouth and at Deptford. He was initially appointed as a draughtsman to copy Humphreys' draught to be sent to the shipyards for the construction of the new ships. However, Fox expressed concerns over the large dimensions (specifically the length and sharpness of the bow) of Humphreys' design that led to considerable animosity between the two men. Humphreys accused Fox of altering his draught and changing features of his design during copying. As a result, Fox was reassigned to work in the mould loft, a large building or floor where the ship's lines are laid down full size in chalk. Patterns (moulds) are made from them for the ship's timbers to be cut out and assembled, and here Fox would have the opportunity to alter the shape of the moulds. There has been no resolution to the controversy, and the origin of the ship's actual lines was fiercely debated in the newspapers as late as 1827.

There was a shortage of skilled shipwrights in the United States and Fox was not dismissed; indeed, he was later appointed as the naval constructor to build *Chesapeake* in Gosport, Virginia. During the construction of *Chesapeake*, he altered Humphreys' design to his own liking, adding fuel to the controversy over *Constitution*'s lines. However, why he altered *Chesapeake*'s design to make it significantly smaller is not clear, although it received approval from the Secretary of the Navy. One of the reasons may have been the result of a timber shortage but he may simply have built the ship to dimensions he thought appropriate for a frigate. The remaining ships were largely built to Humphreys' draught at yards across the northern seaboard, although *Constellation* and *Congress* were scaled-down versions. *President* was assigned to Christian Berg at New York, New York; *United States* under Joshua Humphreys at Philadelphia Pennsylvania; *Congress* to Kittery, Maine, under James Hackett; and *Constellation* to Baltimore, Maryland under David Stodder. *Constitution* was assigned to Edmund Hartt's yard in Boston, Massachusetts. George Claghorn was appointed as the naval constructor and John T Morgan as master shipwright. Samuel Nicholson, *Constitution*'s prospective first captain, oversaw the build. The total funds allocated for the six frigates was $688,888.82 (approximately $19.3 million in 2024).

As built, *Constitution*'s hull was 21 inches (530 mm) thick with a length between perpendiculars of 175ft (53m) and beam of 43ft 6in (13.26m). Sixty acres (24 ha) of pine, oak, and notably southern *Quercus virginiana* (known as 'live oak') was used for the for the hull frames. The wood from this species is extremely dense and its irregular grain renders it resistant to pressure and weight. This wood was harvested largely by slave labour from the humid swamps of the southern states, leading the American historian Carl Herzog (2022) to observe that '... enslaved people were essential to the construction of naval warships built to secure the very American freedoms they were denied ...'. The long straight trunks of red and white oak were used for her planking, and white oak for her keel. Masts and deck planks were made from pine.

By December 1795 Humphreys reported:

> ... The keel is completed and laid on the blocks. The pieces are scarfed and bolted to each other in the best manner. The stern frame is now completing, and will be soon ready to raise. The stern is also putting together, every part being worked to the moulds. About two-thirds of the live oak timbers have been received, and are all worked agreeable to the moulds; great part of those timbers are bolted together in frames, and are ready to put into the ship, but some of the principal pieces for the frames have not yet arrived. All the gun deck and lower deck beams are procured and ready for delivery, and the plank for those decks are received into the yard. The plank for the outside and ceiling are also received and are now seasoning. The copper is all in the public stores. The masts, bowsprit, yards, and other spars, all are ready for working. The bitts for the cables, coamings for the hatchways, partners for the masts, are all ready. The caboose, with a forge, hearth, armorer's tools, spare coppers, boilers, etc, are all complete. Most of the ironwork is in great forwardness. All the necessary contracts are entered into by agent, and the articles contracted for are arriving daily ... (cited from Martin, 1997, p12).

In March 1796 a treaty was signed with the Bey of Algiers Moustapha ben Sliman El-Ouznadji, and in accordance with the Naval Act of 1794 all work was to be stopped on the ships. However, the construction of *Constitution*, *Constellation*, and *United States* was well advanced and allowed to complete. *Constitution*'s launch was scheduled for 20 September 1797, but the ship refused to slide down the ways into the water. The following day a second attempt got the hull to move to the edge of the water. A month later, on 21 October, she finally entered the water after the inclination of the slipway was increased. Her first

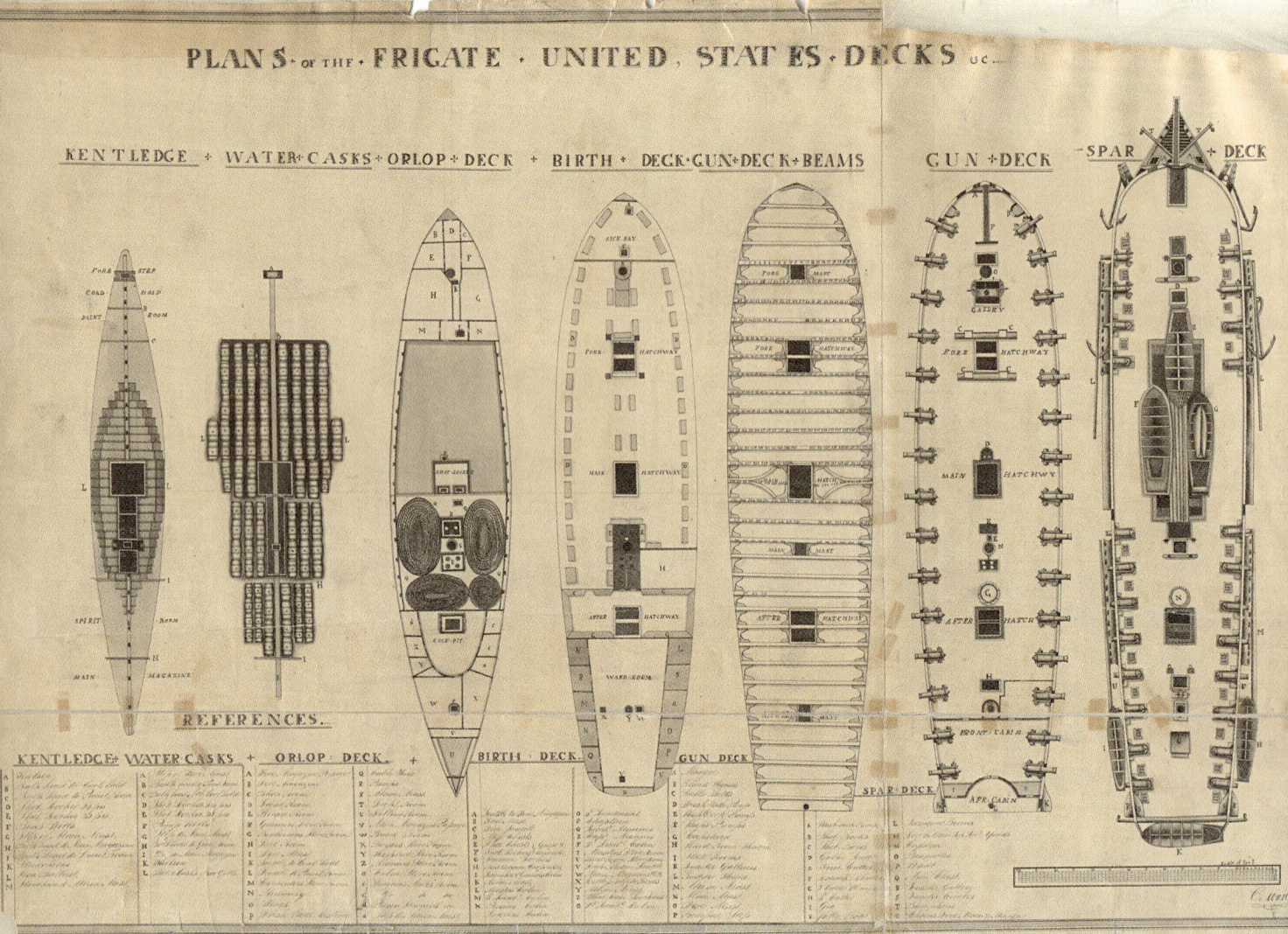

Deck plans of the *United States* (drawn by Charles Ware in 1818). This ship was built to the same Humphreys draught as *Constitution*. (NARA)

captain, Nicholson, was keen to be the first to hoist the ship's colours but because he had routinely berated the dockyard workers and was well despised, two dockyard workers quietly crept aboard the ship to deprive him of this honour.

Constitution spent the next year fitting out until she was ready for her first cruise on 22 July 1798. Stephen Higginson, the Naval Agent in Boston, made some interesting observations on the crew. He described Nicholson as 'a rough blustering Tar merely' but a good seaman; 2nd Lt John Cordis as 'deficient at every point' and 'intemperate' and of the surgeon, William Read, 'there is not a man in this town who would trust the life of a dog in his hands'. (cited in Martin, 1997, pp19–20). Nicholson's unpopularity in Boston had seamen preferring to sign onto other ships and *Constitution* remained in port much longer than anticipated. On 2 July, Nicholson was finally able to set sail for the first time for the King's Road (now known as President's Road) and anchored his ship there to deter his crew from desertion and complete the loading of provisions, powder, and shot from Castle Island. Her final cost was $302,718.84 (about $7.6 million in 2024).

Career Highlights

THE UNDECLARED QUASI WAR WITH FRANCE

With the French Revolution in 1789, the new revolutionary government (Le Consulat), declared war on neighbouring monarchies to spread revolutionary ideas across Europe. For the United States, Le Consulat demanded that the 'Treaties of Alliance' and 'Amity and Commerce' were to continue in perpetuity. The United States objected and unsuccessfully argued that these treaties were rendered void with the beheading of Louis XVI, and that the United States had no agreements with the new French republic. Consistent with this position, in 1793 the US Congress decided unilaterally to stop the repayment of the French loans. By now, the monarchies of continental Europe, notably Russia, Austria, and Prussia formed a coalition against France. Great Britain joined the coalition to support Royalist revolts in France aimed at restoring the French monarchy and enacted the 'Acts of Trade and Navigation' in support. These acts permitted the Royal Navy to blockade ports of belligerent countries and their allies, and this consequently affected American trade by restricting access to foreign markets for the United States. As for the Americans, they were conflicted about how to deal with France. On the one hand the New England states held pro-British sentiments and wanted neutrality so the blockade would not apply to them; but the Southern states, despite holding anti-British and pro-French sympathies, feared that French revolutionary zeal would ignite a movement to emancipate the slaves whose labour drove the economy of the American South.

After intense negotiation, the French indicated they would accept a form of 'benevolent neutrality' that would allow French privateers access to American ports and the right to sell captured British ships in American prize courts but not *vice versa*. However, the United States viewed neutrality as providing the same privileges to all, and in frustration at French intransigence, opened direct negotiations with Great Britain. On 29 February 1796, the 'Jay Treaty' was ratified where the British agreed to end discrimination against American commerce and the United States would prohibit the outfitting of privateers by Britain's enemies in American ports. The French naturally objected and in response issued decrees permitting French privateers to take all merchant ships, regardless of nationality, sailing in American waters. They roamed freely and from October 1796 to June 1797 reportedly captured 316 American ships with trade losses amounting to $12 to $15 million ($28.3 to $36.2 million in 2024 dollars). Despite these losses, it was recognised that the impact of the French decrees would have been much worse if not for the blockades of French ports by the Royal Navy and the informal cooperation that allowed American and British merchant ships to join each other's convoys.

The French subsequently increased the pressure on 2 March 1797 by issuing a decree permitting the seizure of *any* neutral shipping without a *role d'equipage* (a crew muster sheet that listed the nationalities of each crewman), knowing that it was extremely uncommon for American merchantman to carry such a document. In response, on 12 June 1798, *Constitution*'s Captain Nicholson was finally ordered 'to secure from the Depradations [sic] of the French Cruisers, the principal Ports of New Hampshire, Massachusetts, & Rhode Island, & to pay some attention to that of New York', authorising the capture of French armed vessels anywhere on the high seas and territorial waters (from Martin, 1997). *Constitution* took up station around major Caribbean trading ports and her presence added to the significant deterrence provided by the British naval presence in the region. On 30 September 1800, Napoléon Bonaparte became *Premier Consul* of the French Republic and decided to end the Quasi War because the actions of the Royal Navy and its unofficial allies had taken a serious toll on French West Indies trade. Bonaparte's *convention* (order) recognised the neutrality of the United States and formally ended the alliances signed in 1778 – but he also refused to provide any compensation for the $20 million (about $489.6 million in 2024) claimed in damages by the United States for lost shipping.

THE FIRST BARBARY WAR

In 1801 Yusuf Qaramanli, Pasha and Bey of Tripoli, demanded an increase to the tribute paid by the United States after he discovered he was being paid less than the Bey of Algiers. He demanded an immediate payment of $250,000.00 (approximately

$6.1 million in 2024) and, when refused, declared war on the United States. The American response came early the following year by sending two naval squadrons to Tripoli as a show of force and to protect American shipping in the area. By September 1803 Commodore Edward Preble, now in command of Constitution, moved to blockade the major harbours around Tripoli, but his blockade did not begin well. On 31 October the *Philadelphia* (a 36-gun frigate) ran aground on a reef while pursuing a corsair into Tripoli harbour. Whilst trying to free the ship, the Tripolitans attacked and the Americans were forced to surrender. *Philadelphia* was refloated and taken into Tripoli, but Preble realised that if she was refitted and brought into the Bey's service it would shift the balance of power against the Americans, compelling him to attempt recapture or destruction of the ship. In February 1804 a naval crew led by Lieutenant Stephen Decatur from *Constitution* slipped into Tripoli harbour in the *Intrepid*, a ketch previously captured from the Tripolitans, guided by a Sicilian pilot who knew the harbour. Decatur and his crew remained hidden until they were alongside the *Philadelphia* when they boarded and overwhelmed the small Tripolitan crew. Decatur deemed it too difficult to sail her out, so she was set alight.

However, the blockade dragged on and Preble decided to take more offensive action. In August 1804 the *Constitution*, the brigs *Argus* (2 x 12-pounder guns and 8 x 24-pounder carronades) and *Syren* (16 x 24-pounder carronades), the schooners *Enterprise* (12 x 6-pounder guns) and *Scourge* (4 x 6-pounder guns and 4 x 4-pounder guns), six gunboats, and two

A detail of a large painting of Co*nstitution* at Tripoli painted by Michel Felice Cornè, one of many portraits of the ship painted by this artist. This depiction differs in many details from his other studies and is notable for its dramatic effect as opposed to being an accurate portrayal of the ship. Note that the ship is shown with a complete battery on the spar deck with no break in the waist bulwarks as modified under Preble's command in 1804. The original is located at the United States Naval Academy. (*Evan Gale Collection*)

Constitution in 1803 by Michel Felice Cornè. There are no guns in the waist, with hammock netting in the conventional frigate fashion instead of solid bulwarks. This was as the ship first went to sea. (*Courtesy of the USS Constitution Museum, Boston*)

bomb ketches directly assaulted Tripoli harbour for several months. *Constitution's* guns focused on the shore batteries while the smaller ships chased corsairs. Despite considerable damage and losses, the Bey remained firm in his demand for ransom and tribute. The deadlock finally ended when the Bey's brother Hamet and his army of Arabs, Christian Greeks and Turkish mercenaries supported by a unit of American Marines defeated Yusef's forces at the Battle of Derna on 26 April 1805. Yusuf had previously deposed his bother Hamet to take control of Tripoli and had even murdered their older brother in front of their mother to seize control.

The capture of Derna leveraged a peace agreement, signed on board *Constitution*, that effectively ended the seizure of American ships, but it did not prevent them from being stopped and inspected simply because other European powers continued to pay tribute. With the treaty in place the *Constitution* was sent to Malta in September for repairs where she collided with *President*, severely damaging her bow, stern, and figurehead. Most of the remaining American ships in the Mediterranean were sent home, but a major conflict in Europe – the Napoleonic Wars – was now well underway, leaving *Constitution*, the schooner *Enterprise*, and the sloop *Hornet* (18 x 32-pounder carronades and 2 x 12-pounder long guns) to spend the next few years observing the Spanish, French and Royal Navy operations against one another.

THE WAR OF 1812

On 21 November 1806, Napoléon, now Emperor of the French, issued the Berlin Decree that all European ports under his control were closed to British ships and that any neutral or French ships would be seized if they visited a British port before entering a continental port. In response, the British issued a series of Orders-in-Council (legislation formally made in the name of the King with the advice and consent of the Privy Council) requiring all neutral ships to obtain a licence before they could sail to Europe. Britain had the means to enforce these orders after neutering the French and Spanish navies at the Battle of Trafalgar in 1805 and continuing the relentless blockades of French and Spanish ports. These Orders-in-Council caused American ships to be stopped and searched, causing outrage in the United States. A particular *cause célèbre* occurred in 1807 when James Barron, commanding the frigate *Chesapeake* (38 guns) who knew he had British deserters on board, refused to submit to searching by the British *Leopard* (50 guns) commanded by Salusbury Pryce Humphreys. When Barron refused to *heave to* (stop or slow down), *Leopard* opened fire, killing 3 and injuring

18 of his crew. The British boarded and seized four deserters. In the United States, such incidents were interpreted as the unlawful impressment of Americans into the Royal Navy.

However, it should be noted that much of the manpower of the American navy and merchant marine was composed of native-born Britons and only a small number were formally naturalised American citizens that carried papers. To make matters worse, the US government was slow at issuing papers and deserters often carried false papers (Lambert, 2012). There is little doubt that the British did seize any person they *suspected* of being a deserter, but it is not widely known that any suspect's papers were sent to Washington for verification. If found genuine, the man would be released, but unfortunately for the man, this verification process could take months or years, and until then he was in service of the King.

The Americans demanded that the Orders-in-Council be rescinded and, embroiled in an existential conflict with Napoléon, Britain did not want a distracting war with the United States. Moreover, the Royal Navy was occupied supporting Lord Arthur Wellesley, the future Duke of Wellington's successful campaigns against the French occupation in Portugal and Spain. Lord Liverpool's government thus rescinded the Orders-in-Council a few days before the US declared war on 18 June 1812. However, President Madison was decidedly anti-British after his experiences in the revolutionary war and decided not to rescind the declaration of war once his demands had been met. He felt that Upper Canada would be an easy conquest – and even believed the Americans would be greeted as liberators. Despite the President's convictions, within the United States the enthusiasm for war was mixed. The Southern states favoured invasion in retaliation for the economic distress caused by the British blockades and for the unsubstantiated perception of British support of the aboriginal peoples resisting American expansion into the West. On the other

Below and opposite: A model of *Constitution* made by her crew and presented to Isaac Hull after their battle with *Guerriere*. This model is the best contemporary reference on the ship's general appearance in 1812. (*Courtesy of the Peabody Essex Museum. Photography by Walter Silver*)

CAREER HIGHLIGHTS 11

A sketch of Constitution drawn by Commodore Rogers in 1812. The ship is shown carrying every conceivable staysail and flying kite, giving a good idea of what the ship may have looked like when pursued by the British squadron in July 1812. (NARA)

hand, the merchants of New England and New York were against war because Britain was the main customer for their goods.

The Escape

With the declaration of war, Constitution, now under Isaac Hull, was tasked with disrupting British shipping. In July 1812, whilst attempting to join a squadron under the command of Commodore Rodgers in President, he sighted five ships off Egg Harbor, New Jersey. Believing them to be Rodgers' squadron set a course to join them. As he drew near in the light winds, he discovered them to be a British squadron composed of the 38-gun frigate Guerriere, commanded by Captain James Dacres, Africa (64 guns) under Captain John Bastard, and three other frigates — Shannon (38 guns) under squadron commodore Philip Broke, the 36-gun Belvidera commanded by Richard Byron, and the 32-gun Aeolus under Captain James Townsend. The ships met at some distance, but all were becalmed by the slight winds. They drifted aimlessly until the breeze picked up for the British ships who began to slowly bear down on Constitution. Hopelessly outgunned, Hull decided he had to escape and ordered two cutters hoisted out to tow the ship forward. About an hour later the British opened fire with bow chasers and Hull replied by cutting away his transom to make room for two stern chasers and returned fire. The British also deployed cutters to tow their ships and soon Shannon began to gain. To counter Shannon's progress, Hull decided to *warp* the ship forward by dropping a small anchor (known as a kedge anchor) far ahead of the ship and haul in the anchor cable using the main capstan to pull the ship ahead. The Constitution's crew tirelessly kedged during the day and night to keep Constitution out of range until the wind picked up over the next day and drew far ahead. The last British ship, Belvidera, abandoned the chase after falling 12 miles astern. Hull headed north for Boston and safety.

Constitution and Guerriere

On 2 August Constitution sailed east searching for British merchantmen along the coasts of Nova Scotia and Newfoundland and stationed herself off Cape Race in the Gulf of the St Lawrence. Here Constitution captured and burned three British merchantmen rather than risk taking them back to an American port. On the 15th, an unnamed American brig, prize to the British sloop Avenger (a converted collier carrying 2 x 9-pounder chase guns and 18 x 24-pounder carronades), was recaptured but Avenger managed to escape.

On the 19 August the British frigate Guerriere was spotted. Guerriere had been captured in 1806 from the French and under the same name brought into the Royal Navy where she commenced active service in 1808. The ship was detached from the squadron that previously chased Constitution to Halifax for a much need refit after months at sea and blockade duty. Her mast steps (socket or base in keel where the bottom of the mast is fixed) were rotten and the hull planking had sprung in places. At 4:30pm the two ships positioned themselves and hoisted their colours, and Dacres allowed any Americans in his crew to quit their guns. On a side note, American writers have often pondered why Dacres would accept battle from such a large and

well-armed foe. The answer lies in the Royal Navy's Articles of War (statutory set of regulations that set out the expectations of officers and men) that clearly state:

XII. Withdrawing or keeping back from fight, &c. *Every person in the fleet, who through cowardice, negligence, or disaffection, shall in time of action withdraw or keep back, or not come into the fight or engagement, or shall not do his utmost to take or destroy every ship which it shall be his duty to engage, and to assist and relieve all and every of His Majesty's ships, or those of his allies, which it shall be his duty to assist and relieve, every such person so offending, and being convicted thereof by the sentence of a court martial, shall suffer death.*

The spirit of this Article was embodied by Horatio Nelson who famously said, 'No captain can do very wrong if he places his ship alongside that of the enemy' and 'Our Country will, I believe, sooner forgive an Officer for attacking his Enemy than for letting it alone.' The US Navy would later

The decoration of the head probably represents the repair received in 1808 after the ship's collision with *President*. It was still in place in 1812. (*Courtesy of the Peabody Essex Museum. Photography by Walter Silver*)

The model's transom shows how it appeared at the time *Constitution* ran from the British squadron. During the chase, the transom was cut by Isaac Hull to make room to mount chase guns, and these cuts were repaired before her encounter with *Guerriere*. After her battle with *Guerriere*, specifically in October 1812 when under the command of William Bainbridge, the stern was repaired and received minor decoration changes including the drops between the windows. (*Courtesy of the Peabody Essex Museum. Photography by Walter Silver*)

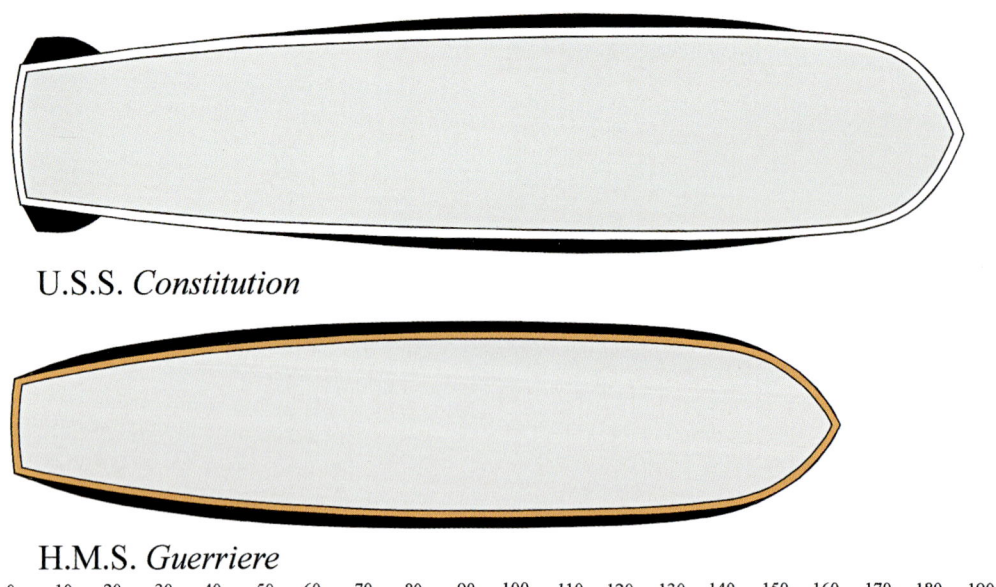

A comparison of the size of *Constitution* and *Guerriere*. Although *Constitution* was classed as a 44-gun ship, she normally carried 56 and her broadside threw 754 pounds of metal. Her crew amounted to 480 sailors and Marines. In contrast, the *Guerriere* was a lightly built French 38-gun frigate that carried 44 guns throwing 526 pounds of metal in British service as a Fifth Rate vessel. At the time of battle the ship was in dire need of refit and en route to Halifax for repairs with her crew of 272 sailors and Marines.

adopt a version of Britain's Articles of War for their own navy.

James Dacres' first-hand account of the battle in a letter to Vice Admiral Herbert Sawyer provides a vivid description (excerpted) of the encounter with *Constitution*:

Boston 7th September 1812

Sir, I am sorry to inform you of the Capture of His Majesty's late Ship *Guerriere* by the American Frigate *Constitution* after a severe action on the 19th of August in Latitude 40.20 N and Longitude 55.00 West. At 2 PM being by the Wind on the starboard Tack, we saw a Sail on our Weather Beam, bearing down on us. At 3 made her out to be a Man of War, beat to Quarters and prepar'd for Action. At 4, She closing fast wore to prevent her raking us. At 4.10 hoisted our Colours and fir'd several shot at her. At 4.20 She hoisted her Colours and return'd our fire. Wore several times, to avoid being raked, Exchanging broadsides. At 5 She clos'd on our Starboard Beam, both keeping up a heavy fire and steering free, his intention being evidently to cross our bow. At 5.20, our Mizen Mast went over the starboard quarter and brought the Ship up in the Wind. The Enemy then plac'd himself on our larboard Bow, raking us, a few only of our bow Guns bearing and his Grape and Riflemen sweeping our Deck. At 5.40 the Ship not answering her helm, he attempted to lay up on board at this time. Mr Grant who commanded the Forecastle was carried below badly wounded. I immediately order'd the Marines and Boarders from the Main Deck; the Master was at this time shot thro the knee, and I receiv'd a severe wound in the back. Lieutenant Kent was leading on the Boarders, when the Ship coming too, we brought some of our bow guns to bear on her and had got clear of our opponent when at 6.20 our Fore and Main Masts went over the side, leaving the Ship a perfect unmanageable Wreck. The Enemy shooting ahead, I was in hopes to clear the Wreck and get the Ship under Command to renew the Action but just as we had clear'd the Wreck our Spritsail yard went and the Enemy having rove new Braces &c, wore round within Pistol Shot to rake us. The Ship laying in the trough of the Sea and rolling her Main Deck Guns under Water and all attempts to get her before the Wind being fruitless, when calling my few remaining officers together, they were all of opinion that any further resistance would be a needless waste of lives, I order'd, though reluctantly, the Colours to be struck. The loss of the Ship is to be ascribed to the early fall of the Mizen Mast which enabled our opponent to choose his position. I am sorry to say we suffered severely in killed and wounded and mostly whilst she lay on our Bow from her Grape and Musketry, in all 15 kill'd and 63 wounded, many of them severely; none of the wounded Officers quitted the Deck till the firing ceas'd. The Frigate prov'd to be the United States Ship *Constitution*, of thirty 24 Pounders on her Main Deck and twenty four 32 Pounders and two 18 Pounders on her Upper Deck and 476 Men – her loss in comparison with ours was triffling, about twenty, the first Lieutenant of Marines and eight killed and first Lieutenant and Master of the Ship and eleven Men wounded, her lower Masts badly wounded; and stern much shattered and very much cut up about the Rigging. The *Guerriere* was so cut up, that all attempts to get her in would have been useless. As soon as the wounded were got out of her, they set her on fire, and I feel it my duty to state that the conduct of Captain Hull and his

Officers to our Men has been that of a brave Enemy, the greatest care being taken to prevent our Men losing the smallest trifle, and the greatest attention being paid to the wounded who through the attention ... I hope, in considering the circumstances, you will think the Ship entrusted to my charge was properly defended; the unfortunate loss of our Masts, the absence of the third lieutenant, second Lieutenant of Marines, three Midshipmen, and twenty four Men considerably weakened our Crew, and we only muster'd at Quarters 244 Men and 19 Boys, on coming into action; the Enemy had such an advantage from his Marines and Riflemen, when close and his superior sailing enabled him to choose his distance. I enclose herewith a List of killed and wounded on board the *Guerriere* and have the Honor to be Sir, Your most obedient &c.

Sign'd J R Dacres

(British National Archives, Admiralty 1/502, Part 4, 541–545).

Off the Coast of Brazil

Five months after her encounter with *Guerriere*, *Constitution* was now under the command of Captain William Bainbridge. Off the coast of Brazil, she encountered and engaged *Java* under the command of Captain Henry Lambert on 29 December 1812. *Java* was a typically lightly built French frigate, originally the *Renommée* of 38 guns captured in 1809 and brought into Royal Navy service.

This excerpt from the journal kept by Commodore Bainbridge describes the action between *Constitution* and *Java*.

Wednesday 30th Decr 1812 Lat 13°.06 South and Long. 38 West, 10 leagues from the Coast of Brazils – Commences with clear weather & moderate breezes From E.N.E. hoisted our Ensign and Pendant. At 15 minutes past Meridian the strange sail hoisted her Colours and English Ensign, having a signal flying at her main at 1.26 P.M. being sufficiently from the land and finding the ship to be an English Frigate, took in the mainsail & Royal, tacked Ship and stood for the enemy at 1.50 P.M. the enemy bore down with the intention of raking us, which we avoided by wearing – at 2 P.M. the enemy being within half a mile of us and to windward and having hauled down his colours (excepting a Union Jack at the mizen masthead) induced

The battle between *Constitution* and *Guerriere* painted by Michel Felice Cornè. (NARA)

me to give orders to the officer of the 3rd division to fire one Gun ahead of the enemy to make him show his colours, which being done, brought on a fire from us of the whole broadside on which the enemy hoisted his colours and immediately returned our fire – A general action with round & grape then commenced, the enemy keeping at a much greater distance than I wished but could not bring him to closer action without exposing ourselves to several rakes – Considerable maneuvers were made by both vessels to rake and avoid being raked. The following minutes were taken during the action – at 2.10 P.M. – Commenced the action in good Grape & Cannister distance the enemy to windward (but much further than I wished) 2.30. Our wheel was shot entirely away 2.40. determined to close with the enemy notwithstanding his raking, set the fore & main sail & luffed up to close him. 2.50 The enemies boom got foul our Mizen Rigging. 3.00 The Heel of the Enemies Bowsprit & Jib boom shot away by us. 3.05 Shot away the Enemies Foremast by the board 3.40 Shot away Gaff & spanker boom 3.55 Shot away his mizen [sic] mast nearly by the board 4.05 Having silence the fire of the enemy completely and his colours in main rigging being down, supposed he had struck, then hauled aboard the courses to shoot ahead to repair our rigging which was extremely cut, leaving the enemy a complete wreck. Soon after discovered that the enemies flag was still flying – Hove too to repair some of our damage 4.20. The enemies Main Mast went nearly by the board 4.50. Got very close to the enemy in a very effective Raking position athwart his bows and was at the very instance of raking him when he most prudently struck his flag, for had he suffered the broadside to have raked him, his additional loss must have been extremely great as he laid an unmanageable wreck upon the water – after the enemy had struck wore ship and reefed the topsails, then hoisted out one of the only two remaining boats we had left out of 8 and sent Lieut Parker 1st of the Constitution to take possession of the enemy, which proved to be H.B.M. [His Britannic Majesty's] Frigate Java rated 38 but carried 49 guns and manned with upwards of 400 men commanded by Capt Lambert a very distinguished officer who lay mortally wounded. The Action continued from the commencemt to the end of the Fire 1h.55m...

Monday 31st December 1812 All these 24 hours backing wearing and laying too, keeping our position near the prize – Receiving the prisoners & wounded on board – employed in repairing our damage in the rigging – Spars, Sails & Hull, which is considerable – several shot holes through the Hull, on and above the waterline – Quarter deck bulwark very much shot – Rudder chains shot off – several shots

The *Constitution* and *Java* action painted by Michel Felice Cornè. Apart from conflating different stages of the engagement, the size of the British ship is greatly exaggerated. (NARA)

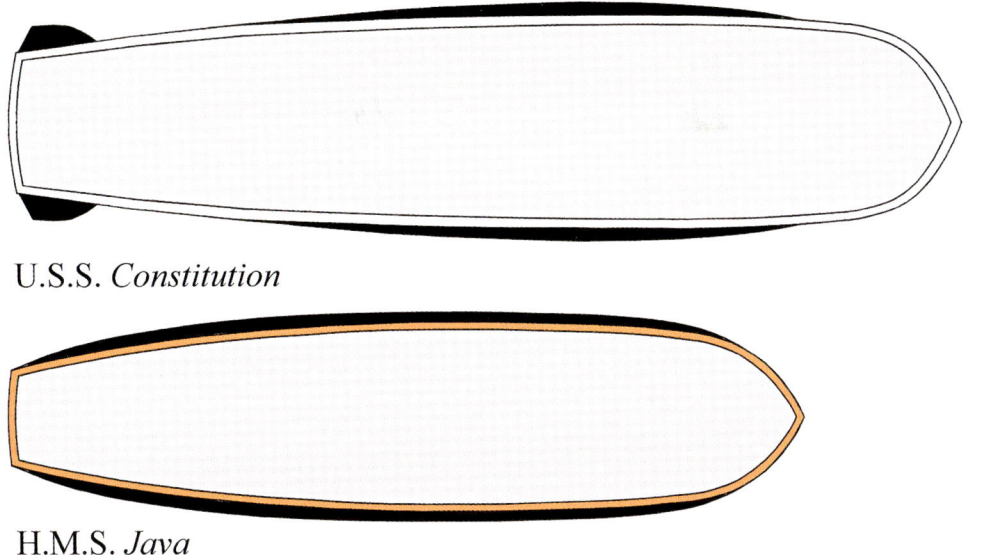

A comparison of the size of *Constitution* and *Java*. *Java* was the captured French frigate *Renommée* brought into Royal Navy service as a Fifth Rate vessel. The ship could throw a broadside of 535 pounds compared to *Constitution*'s 754 pounds. At the time of battle, *Java*'s crew of 426 was raw and inexperienced compared to *Constitution*'s by now seasoned and battle-hardened crew of 475.

through the Cutwater and one through the rudder – Fore & mizen mast shot through – Main Topmast 1/3 cut through, Main Topsail Mast Yard above 12 feet from the end shot away – Spanker boom, Topsail Mast & Gaff shot through & through – Jib boom wounded – Spars in our channels very much shot, many entirely ruined – All boats but 2 greatly shot – our sail very much injured so as to require bending others – The rigging greatly cut to pieces – One of the Carronades injured on the Quarter Deck Compass rails and Binnicals all shot away – One Ridge Line & Hammock very much injured – received the wheel from the Java and fitted it on board of us. Lat 13°54′ S Long 36 D .12′. W Wm Bainbridge

(From Bainbridge's Account of the Engagement with HMS *Java*, USS *Constitution* Museum Collection [2361.1])

The British account is contained in a letter by Lieutenant Chads to Secretary of the Admiralty John W. Croker (excerpted):

United States Frigate Constitution off St Salvador Decr 31st 1812

Sir

It is with deep regret that I write you for the information of the Lords Commissioners of the Admiralty that His Majesty's Ship Java is no more, after sustaining an action on the 29th Inst for several hours with the American Frigate Constitution which resulted in the Capture and ultimate destruction of His Majestys Ship. Captain Lambert being dangerously wounded in the height of the Action, the melancholy task of writing the detail devolves on me.

On the morning of the 29th inst at 8 AM off St Salvador (Coast of Brazil) the wind at NE. we perceived a strange sail, made all sail in chace and soon made her out to be a large Frigate; at noon prepared for action the chace not answering our private Signals and backing towards us under easy sail; when about four miles distant she made a signal and immediately tacked and made all sail away upon the wind, we soon found we had the advantage of her in sailing and came up with her fast when she hoisted American Colours. she then bore about three Points on our lee bow at 1:50 PM the Enemy shortened Sail upon which we bore down upon her, at 2:10 when about half a mile distant she opened her fire giving us her larboard broad-side which was not returned till we were close on her weather bow; both Ships now manoeuvred to obtain advantageous positions; our opponent evidently avoiding close action and firing high to disable our masts in which he succeeded too well having shot away the head of our bowsprit with the Jib boom and our running rigging so much cut as to prevent our preserving the weather gage At 3:5 finding the Enemys raking fire extreemly heavy Captain Lambert ordered the Ship to be laid on board, in which we should have succeeded had not our foremast been shot away at this moment, the remains of our bowsprit passing over his taffrail, shortly after this the main topmast went leaving the Ship totally unmanageable with most of our Starboard Guns rendered useless from the wreck laying over them At 3:30 our Gallant Captain received a dangerous wound in the breast and was carried below, from this time we could not fire more than two or three guns until 4:15 when our Mizen mast was shot away the Ship then fell off a little

Ink and watercolour diagram of the battle between *Constitution* and *Java* drawn by *Constitution*'s Master's Mate Charles Waldo who was stationed on the main fighting top during the battle. Waldo's drawing differs from Commodore Bainbridge's official account of the battle where it shows *Java* crossing *Constitution*'s stern and raking the ship early on. Waldo's diagram also names the British Lieutenant Henrie Ducie Chads at the bottom, so he may have copied Chads' own diagram of the battle, or discussed it with him in the sick bay, as both were injured in the battle. (*NARA/USS Constitution Museum*)

and brought many of our Starboard Guns to bear, the Enemy's rigging was so much cut that he could not now avoid shooting ahead which brought us fairly Broadside and Broadside. Our Main yard now went in the slings both ships continued engaged in this manner till 4:35 we frequently on fire in consequence of the wreck laying on the side engaged. Our opponent now made sail ahead out of Gun shot where he remained an hour repairing his damages leaving us an unmanageable wreck with only the mainmast left, and that tottering; Every exertion was made by us during his interval to place this Ship in a state to renew the action. We succeeded in clearing the wreck of our Masts from our Guns. a Sail was set on the stumps of the Foremast & Bowsprit the weather half of the Main Yard remaining aloft, the main tack was got forward in the hope of getting the Ship before the Wind, our helm being still perfect. the effort unfortunately proved ineffectual from the Main mast falling over the side from the heavy rolling of the Ship, which nearly covered the whole of our Starboard Guns. We still waited the attack of the Enemy, he now standing toward us for that purpose. On his coming nearly within hail of us & from his manoeuvre perceiving he intended a position a head where he could rake us without a possibility of our returning a shot. I then consulted the Officers who agreed with myself that on having a great part of our Crew killed & wounded our Bowsprit and three masts gone, several guns useless, we should not be justified in waisting the lives of more of those remaining whom I hope their Lordships & Country will think have bravely defended His Majestys Ship. Under these circumstances, however reluctantly at 5:50 our Colours were lowered from the Stump of the Mizen Mast and we were taken possession a little after 6. by the American Frigate Constitution commanded by Commodore Bainbridge who immediately after ascertaining the state of the Ship resolved on burning her which we had the satisfaction of seeing done as soon as the Wounded were removed ... I hope their Lordships will not think the British Flag tarnished although success has not attended us ...

I cannot conclude this letter without expressing my grateful acknowledgement thus publicly for the generous treatment Captain Lambert and his Officers have experienced from our Gallant Enemy Commodore Bainbridge and his Officers. I have the honor to be [&c.]

W [H] D Chads, 1st Lieut
of His Majestys late Ship Java

To John Wilson Croker Esquire
Secretary
Admiralty.

PS. The Constitution has also suffered severly, both in her rigging and men having her Fore and Mizen masts, main topmast, both main topsailyards, Spanker boom, Gaff & trysail mast badly

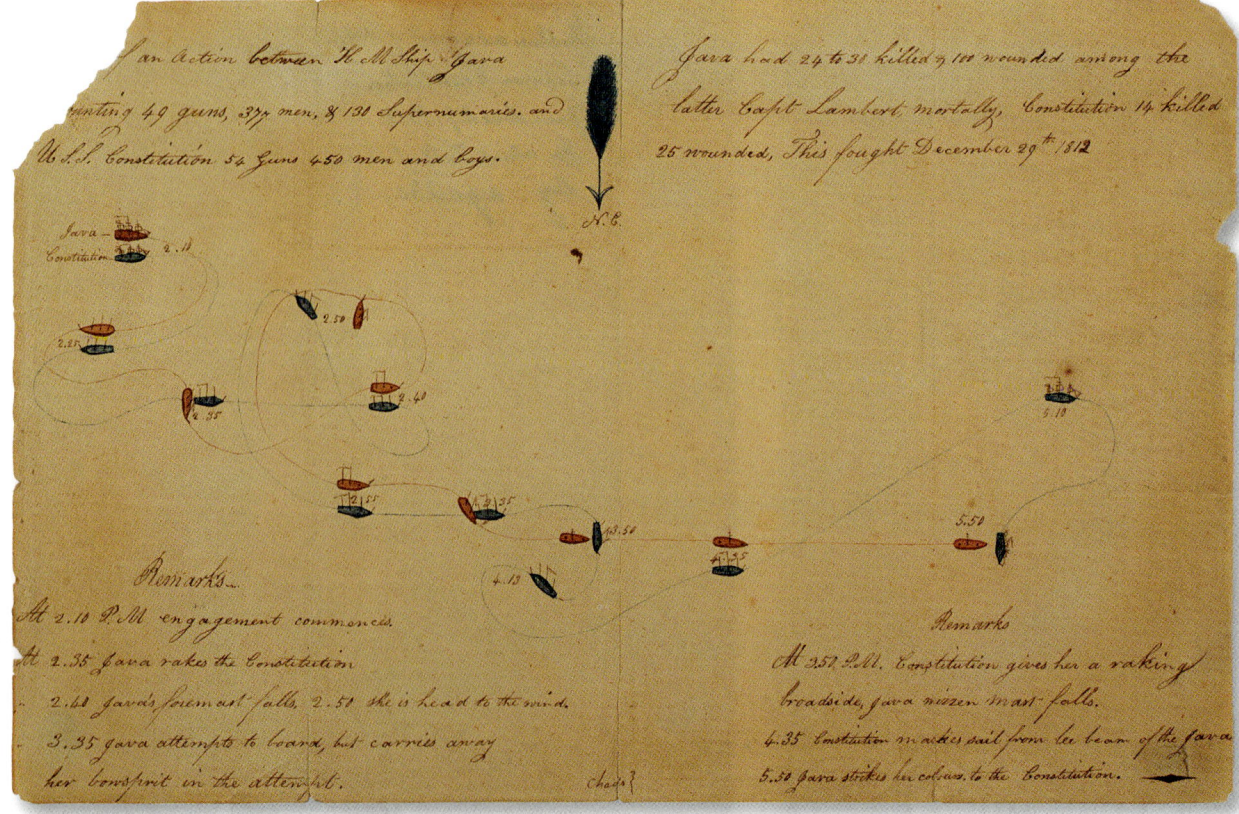

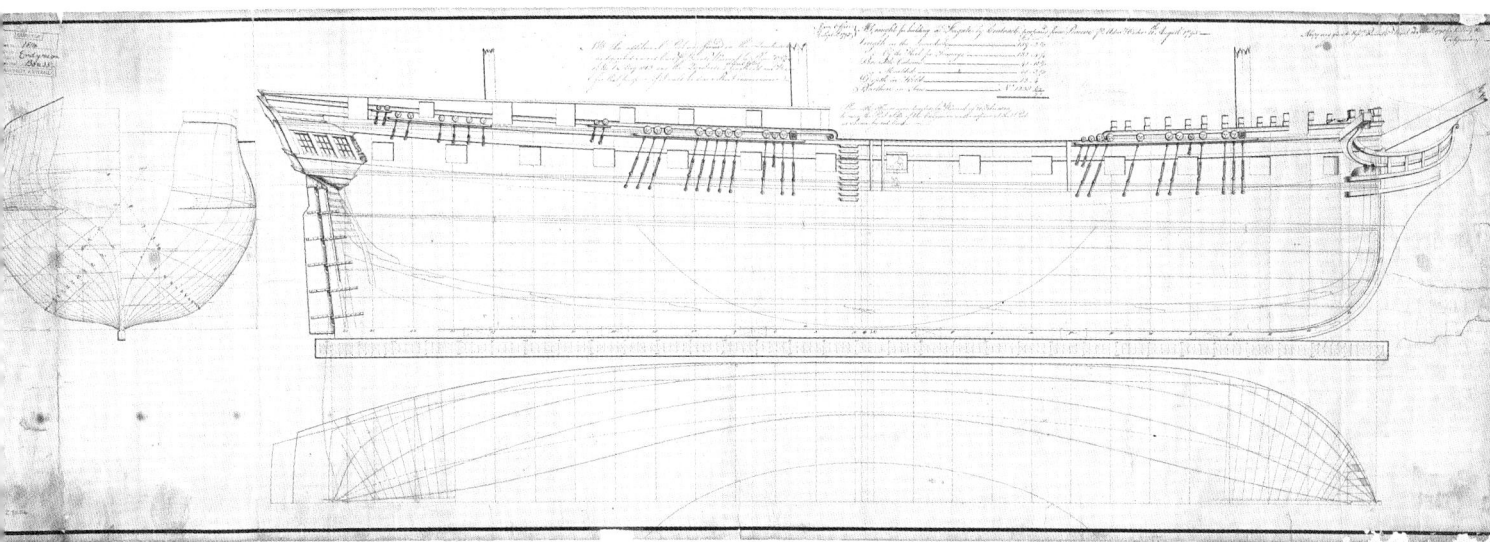

shot, and the greatest part of the standing rigging very much damaged with ten men killed. The Commodore, 5 Lieuts and 46 men wounded four of whom are since dead.

(British National Archives, Admiralty 1/5435.)

The Unnecessary Battle
The defeat of Imperial France and Napoléon's exile to Elba on 11 April 1814 signalled the end of the Napoleonic Wars. For the Americans, the invasion of Canada had not gone well. For two years a small garrison of British regulars, local militia, and Aboriginal First Nations had defeated the invading Americans at virtually every major engagement. The American record at sea as commerce raiders was equally disappointing as it failed to fatally damage British trade. The single-ship victories by *Constitution* and her sister ship *United States* (which defeated the much smaller *Macedonian* of 38 guns on 30 October 1812) were the only bright spots, and as such were wildly celebrated, but they had no significant impact on the war. Indeed, the record of *Constitution* and her sisters, considering their size and scantlings, was at best middling. *Chesapeake* was taken as a prize by *Shannon* commanded by Captain Phillip Broke on 1 June 1813; *President* was blockaded in New York harbour and captured on 15 January 1815, by *Endymion* under Captain Henry Hope. *Constellation* was blockaded at Hampton Roads, Virginia for most of the war. *Congress* successfully captured several British merchant ships but lack of spares and materials for her repair resulted in her being taken out of service in late 1813.

On land, by 1814, British troops had burned Washington in revenge for the American burning of York (now Toronto) and had made successful incursions into Maine. The Americans were desirous to end their disastrous war, especially now that the defeat of France allowed Britain to muster significant land and naval forces for North America. The British also wanted this distracting war to end so they could focus on the establishment of stable government for a defeated France – a prudent policy given that Napoléon was to successfully escape from Elba in March 1815 and attempt to mobilise France, a campaign that finally ended on the field of Waterloo. For all involved, President Madison's ill-fated war to annex the Canadas ended with the signing of the Treaty of Ghent on Christmas Eve 1814 where all agreed to go

Draught of *Endymion* which captured *President*. Armed with 24-pounders, *Endymion* was one of very few British frigates that might be considered a match for the big US 44s, although she was nevertheless smaller and carried fewer guns. (*National Maritime Museum, London J5180*)

Draught of *Constitution*'s sister ship *President* as taken into Royal Navy service. Of the three largest frigates built to Humphreys' draught, *President* was regarded as the best sailer and *United States* the worst. (*National Maritime Museum, London J3607*)

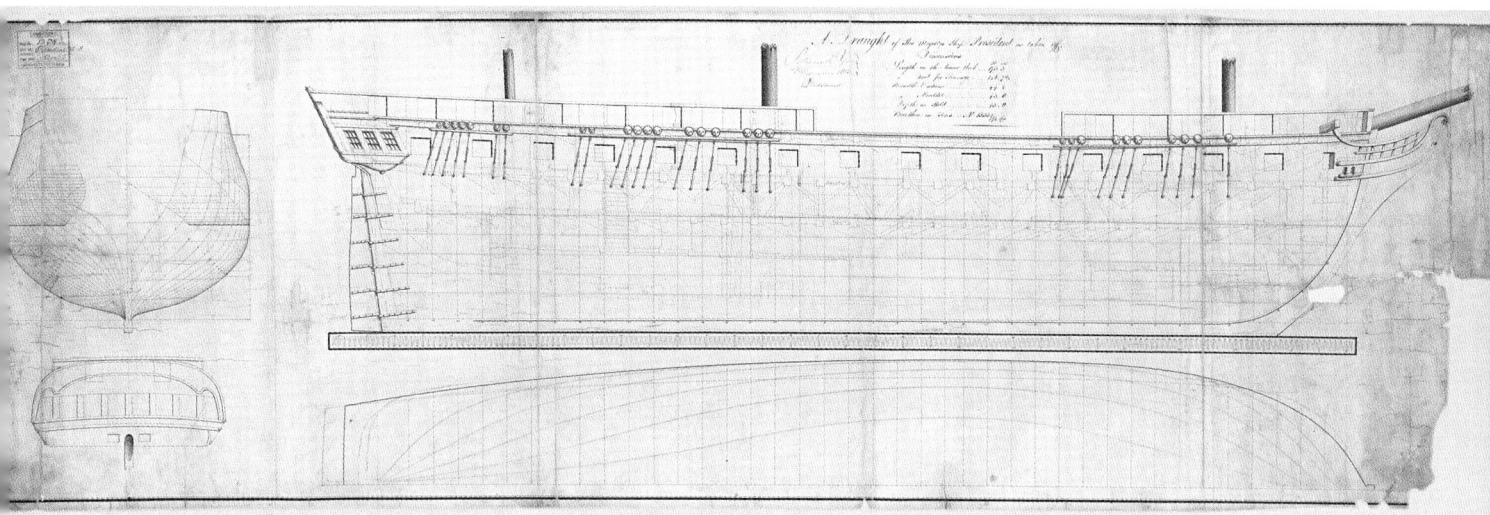

A comparison of the relative sizes of *Constitution* and the Sixth Rates *Cyane* and *Levant*. *Levant*'s main armament was 20 x 32-pounder carronades that could throw 320 pounds of metal, and *Cyane*'s primary armament was 22 x 32-pounder carronades that threw 442 pounds of metal. However, carronades are short-range weapons and because *Constitution* carried 30 x 24-pounder long guns she was able to batter *Cyane* and *Levant* at distance and incapacitate their guns. Once she closed the range, *Constitution* was able to fire her own carronades (22 x 32-pounder carronades). The crews of the two British vessels totalled 310, in contrast, to *Constitution*'s crew of 410 officers and seamen and 41 Marines at the time of their encounter. *Constitution*'s encounters with *Guerriere*, *Java*, *Cyane*, and *Levant* vindicated Humphreys' concept of a large ship that would be able to overpower any smaller enemy ships she was likely to encounter. However, the American frigate's large size and gun batteries did nothing to stop the smaller British ships from offering battle, as Humphreys had envisioned.

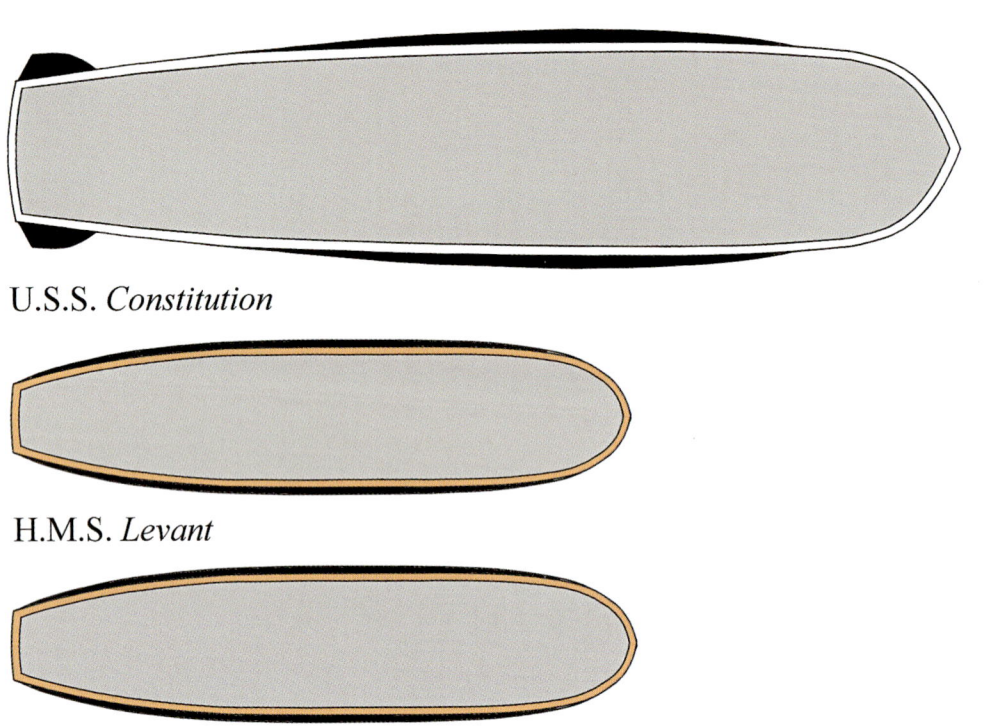

back to boundaries that existed before the American invasion.

Sadly, news that hostilities ended had not reached *Constitution* (now under Captain Charles Stewart), nor the two small British Sixth Rate sloops *Cyane* and *Levant* sailing off the coast of Spain, about one hundred miles east of Madeira, in February 1815. Captain Gordon Thomas Falcon commanded *Cyane*, with the *Levant* under Captain George Douglas.

The British ships were concerned that *Constitution* might intercept a large convoy that had just sailed from Gibraltar, and were determined to prevent it. On 20 February, at 1:00pm Stewart spotted the British ships and set all sail in chase. *Cyane* closed with *Levant* by 5:30pm and hoped to delay battle until after nightfall. However, *Constitution*'s rapid approach forced *Levant* and *Cyane* to form into a line to give battle. At 6:10pm, the action commenced with *Constitution* to windward, *Levant* on her port bow and *Cyane* on her port quarter. The three ships fired broadsides simultaneously but *Cyane*'s shots, being all fired from carronades, fell short, while *Constitution*'s long 24-pounders produced full effect. The *Constitution* ranged ahead to focus on *Levant*. *Cyane* attempted to come up on *Constitution*'s quarter but the move was seen and met with a broadside. *Levant* attempted to wear ship (turn around) to assist *Cyane*, but during the manoeuvre her stern was raked twice. Despite seriously damaged rigging *Cyane* wore to come between *Levant* and the *Constitution* and was raked by *Constitution*, but she managed to fire a larboard (port) broadside at *Constitution*'s starboard bow. *Constitution* positioned herself on *Cyane*'s rear quarter and was

Constitution's battle with *Cyane* and *Levant*. (*National Maritime Museum, London PU5857*)

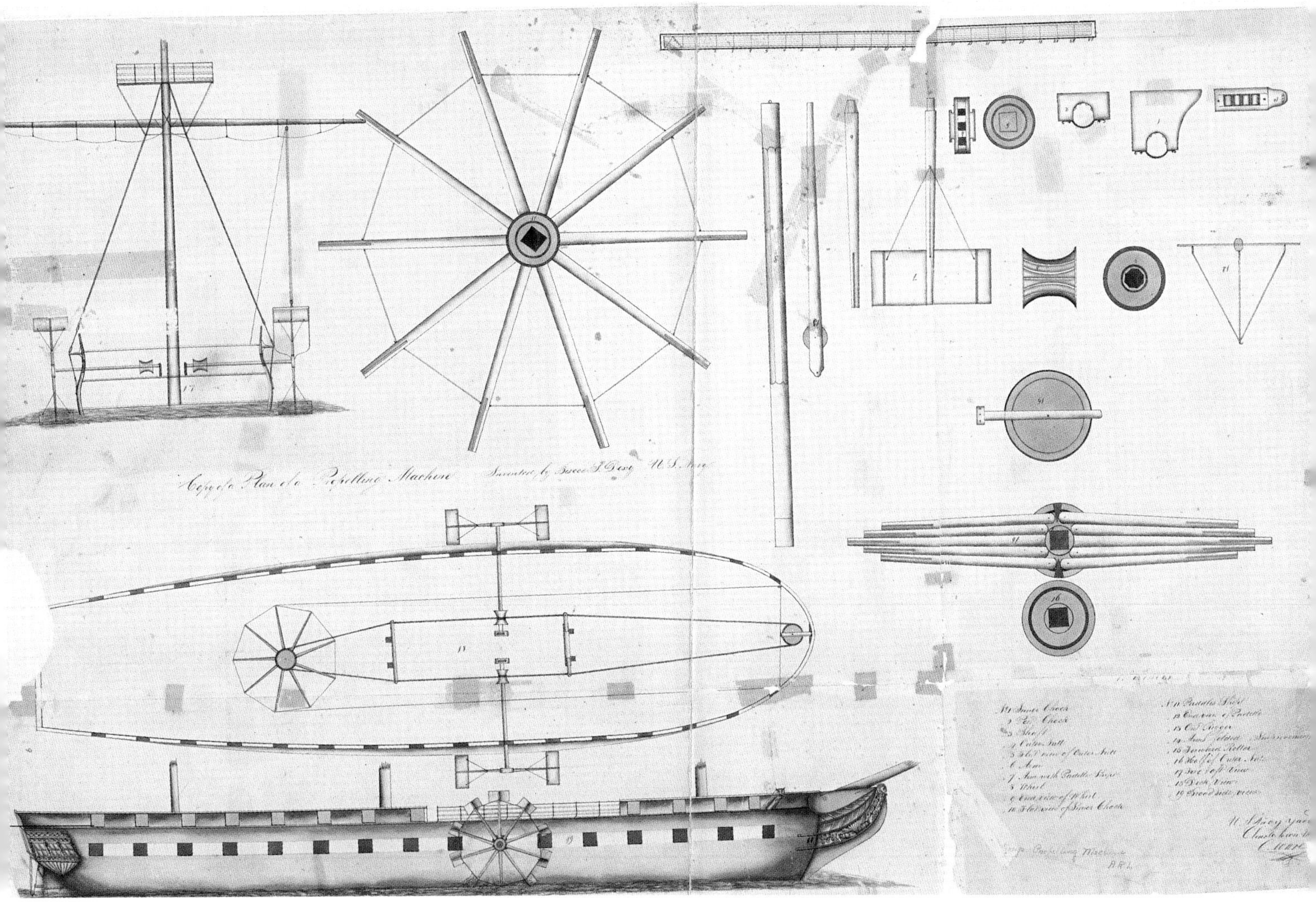

Above: George Ware's drawing of the man-powered 'Propelling Machine' paddlewheel that was only tested a single time on *Constitution* before it was deemed a failure. (*NARA*)

Below: Details of *Constitution* taken from the plans prepared for her 1927 restoration. (*NARA*)

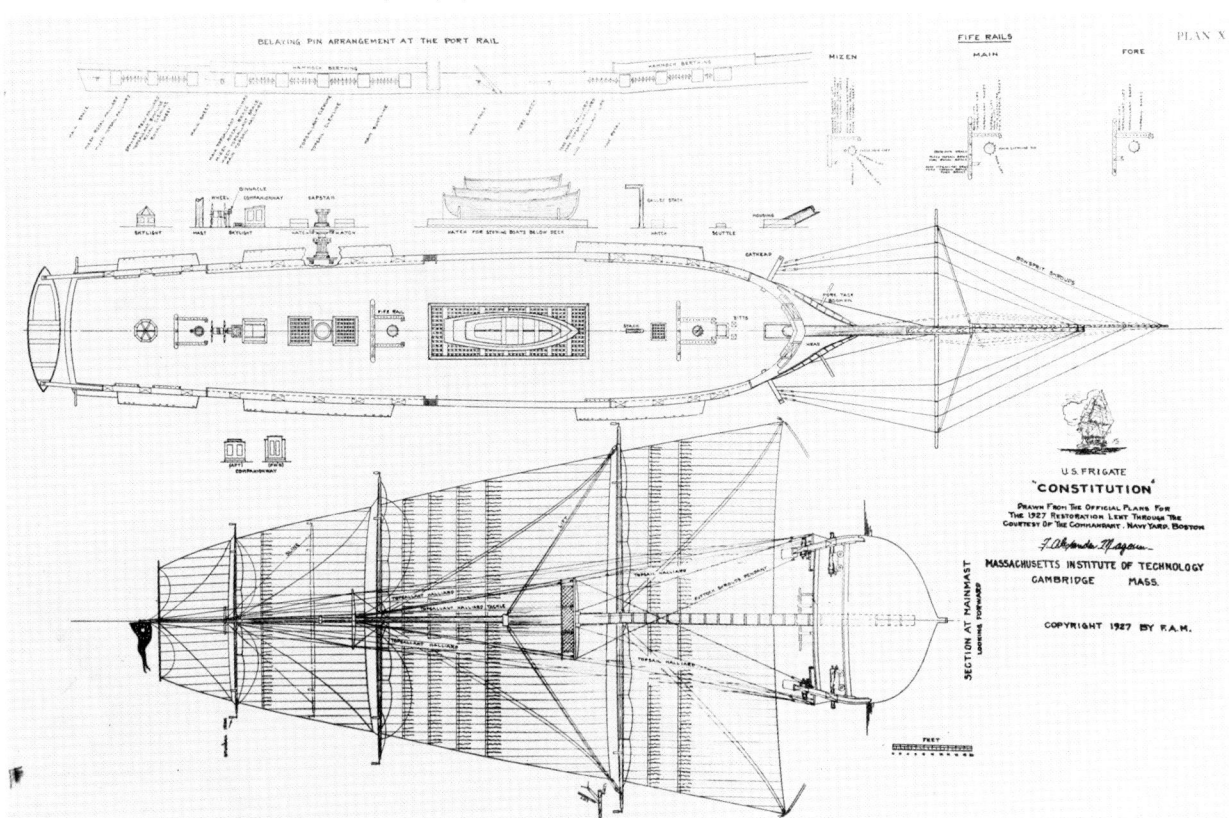

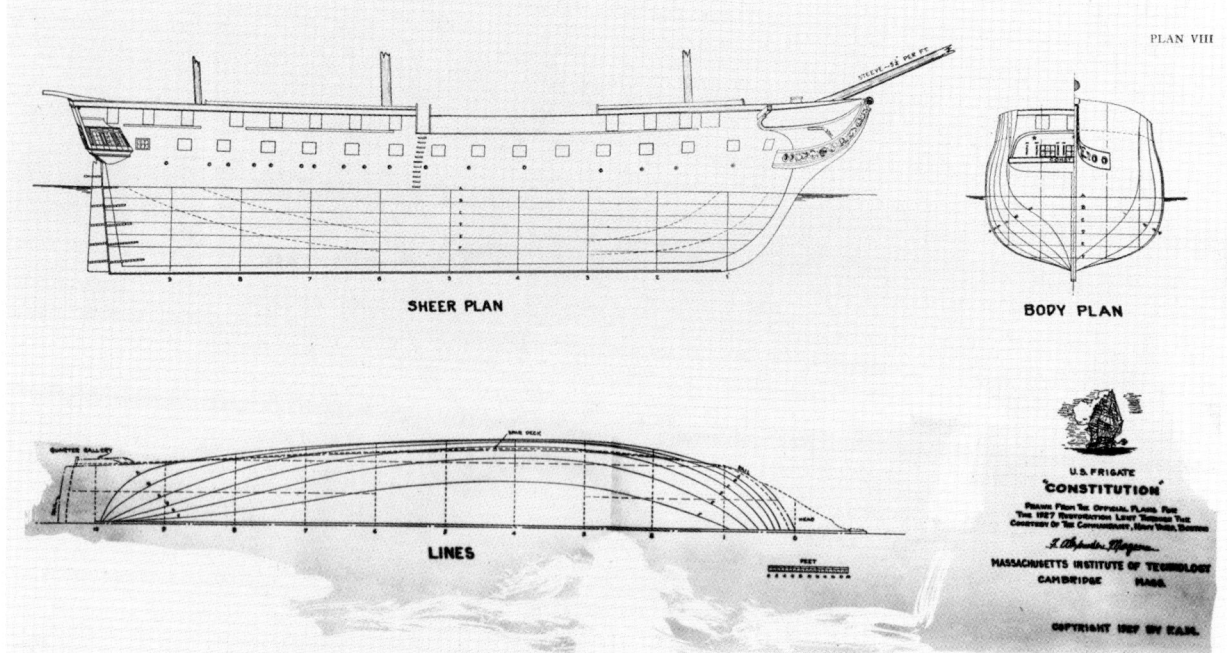

Constitution's hull lines after her 1927 restoration. This saved the ship, but her appearance was changed significantly from her most active years during the First Barbary War and the War of 1812. (*NARA*)

Profile and sail plan of the ship after her 1927 restoration. (*NARA*)

preparing to give the little ship another broadside when she surrendered.

At 8:00pm, Stewart went in pursuit of *Levant*, and at 8:50 discovered the British vessel beating back upwind to re-engage *Constitution* unaware that *Cyane* had struck. The two vessels exchanged broadsides on opposite tacks, when *Levant* attempted to escape the heavier fire but because she was sailing upwind was overtaken and forced to surrendered at 9:30pm. Despite the loss of *Cyane* and *Levant*, the Gibraltar convoy escaped unscathed. On 7 March, *Constitution* and her prizes were discovered in Porto-Praya harbour, Cape Verde by the British 50-gun ships *Leander* (Captain Sir George Collier) and *Newcastle* (Captain Lord George Stuart) and the 40-gun frigate *Acasta* (Captain Alexander Kerr). *Constitution* and her prizes fled the harbour and *Constitution* was forced to lighten ship to outrun the British squadron and managed to escape with *Cyane*, but *Acasta* recaptured *Levant*. Stewart released his prisoners in Brazil and upon reaching Porto Rico he learned that the war had

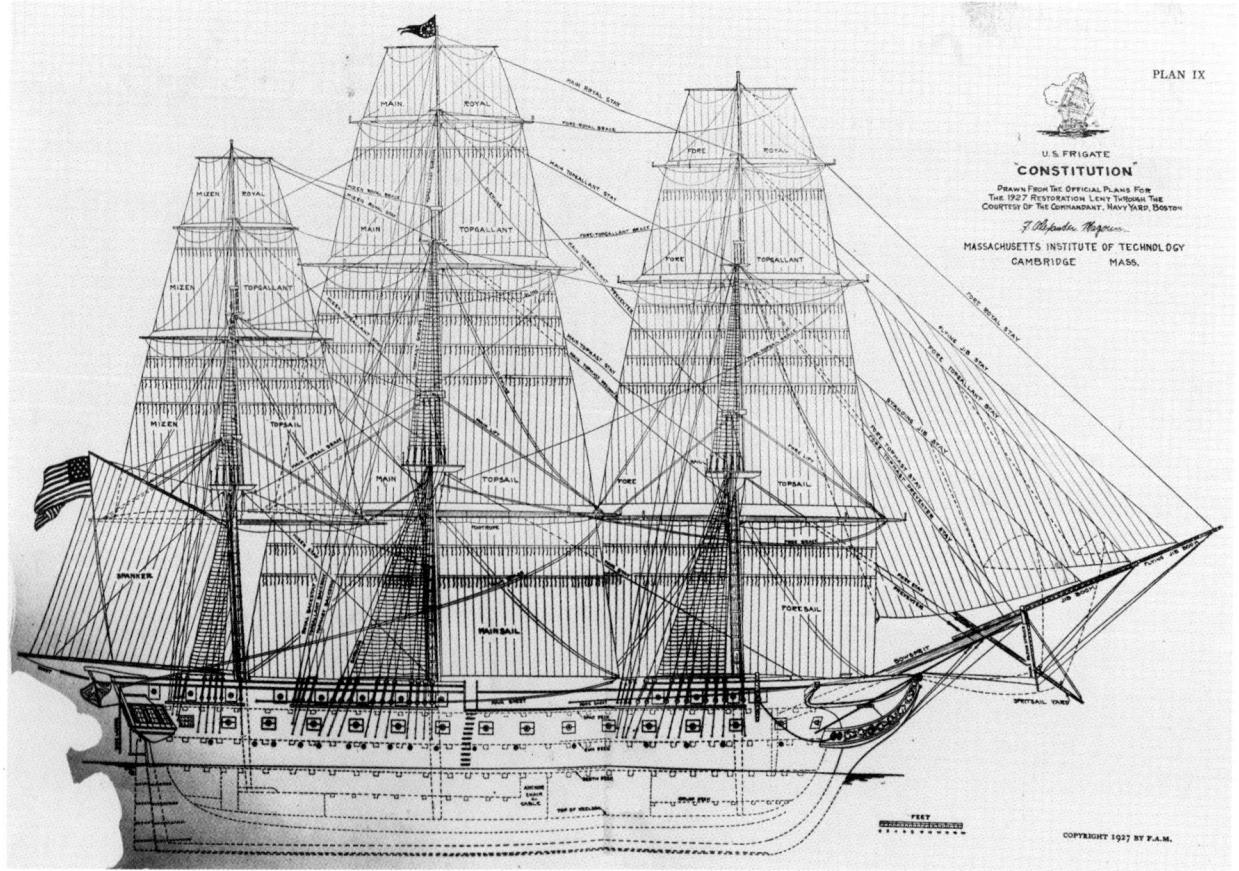

Colourised portrait of *Constitution* after her 1927 restoration. (*Author's Collection*)

The head decoration carried by the ship today. (*Evan Gale Collection*)

Constitution in drydock during her 1927 restoration. (*Author's Collection*)

ended. *Cyane* reached New York without incident and was taken into the US Navy. The Portuguese later paid compensation to the United States for their failure to enforce their neutrality which allowed the recapture of *Levant*. So ends the unnecessary battle of a similarly unnecessary war.

Much has been made of *Constitution*'s victories during the War of 1812, and defeating ships of the greatest naval power of the age certainly raised the prestige and morale of the infant US Navy, thus becoming an enduring part of American naval mythology. However, the historical significance of these actions was greatly exaggerated to serve political ends. As Andrew Lambert in his 2012 book *The Challenge: Britain against America in the Naval War of 1812* observed:

> ... In the ultimate act of cultural construction a single ship was deployed to disguise a failed war. While the British soon forgot 1812, they retained enough relics of glory to subvert American claims. Every time an American president used memories of 1812 to threaten Canada,* the British backed their diplomacy with warships called *President*, *Chesapeake*, *Shannon*, and *Endymion*, because they knew the difference between propaganda and power ... (p5).

AN UNEVENTFUL CAREER AND RESTORATION

Constitution moved to Boston, was placed in ordinary in January 1816, and sat out the Second Barbary War that ended the paying of tribute. In the 1820s she became the test bed for man-cranked paddle wheels for when the ship was becalmed that were

---

* *The United States had threatened to invade Canada up until the 1860s because of the Colony's opposition to slavery and for knowingly being the terminus of the secret 'Underground Railroad' by which abolitionists smuggled slaves out of the US.*

deemed a failure. She was sent on a world cruise to show the flag, followed by extended periods of time sitting in reserve. During the American Civil War, *Constitution* was converted to a naval school ship at Annapolis. In 1881 *Constitution* was found unfit for sea and converted into a receiving ship and floating dock. Returned to Boston in September 1897 she was fitted as a receiving ship until 1906 when Naval Constructor Elliot Snow supervised a restoration of the ship. The receiving ship deckhouse was removed, new masts, yards, and rigging installed, and the upper and waist bulwarks lowered to broadly resemble her 1812 appearance.

However, by 1925 *Constitution* had again fallen into a seriously decayed state, including all her framing above the waterline, her masts and rigging, and a 14-inch hog developed in her keel. In 1927 Lieutenant John Lord supervised a new restoration, but he and his dockyard workers jumbled research from multiple periods in the ship's nineteenth-century history, which coupled with preconceived ideas about how the ship should appear resulted in a hull above the waterline that bore little relation to her 1812 appearance. Nevertheless, the ship was saved, and the restored ship made a tour of the United States in 1931 that lasted until 1934, when she was brought to Boston as a museum ship. Subsequent restorations in 1973 and 1992–1996 maintained her 1927 form until the 2007-2010 restoration that brought her appearance closer to her 1812 appearance by lowering her bulwarks back to their height to just above the spar deck gunports; and the waist bulwarks alongside the main hatch were cut open and fitted with hammock cranes. She sailed unassisted for the first time in 116 years on 21 July 1997; it was also to be the last time.

Constitution's transom after her 1927 restoration photographed at Oakland, California during her tour of the United States. (*Author's Collection*)

The museum ship's quarter galleries post-1996 restoration. (*Evan Gale Collection*)

Model Products

REVELL USS *CONSTITUTION* (Kit #5404)   1:196 Scale

First released in 1960, the presence of an Andrew Jackson figurehead on the stem suggests the model represents the ship's appearance *circa* 1834 – but the transom design is from the 1870s. The hull castings are beautifully detailed with scale planking, chainplates and the correct run of copper plating on the underwater hull. The spar deck sports simplified planking detail with no waterway leaving the planks to run unrealistically into points at the end of the deck edge, but the planks do show an authentic *shift of butts* (staggering of plank ends). The main gun deck below the spar deck is not complete, just a plastic shelf moulded into the hull halves to mount the cannon. This ruse gives the impression of a full gun deck when looking through the gunports, but the illusion is spoiled when looking down through the spar deck into blanked off stairwells.

Several small details, such as the binnacle, are omitted, and other parts like the bitts and capstan are heavily moulded.

The armaments are to scale and authentically detailed. The kit anchors are undersized but larger ones are easily made from scratch using the kit parts as a pattern. The ship's boats are moulded open making them easy to detail with frames made from styrene strips. The masts are moulded as a single piece incorporating the lower, upper, topgallant, and royals, with their *caps* (a band placed around the lower mast and around the top mast to hold the top mast in the correct position) and *mast bands* (metal

Below: The kit has been reissued under many different kit boxes. The illustrated instructions included in the 2014 version are far less detailed than those found in the 1979 issue of the kit. (*All model product photos by the author unless credited otherwise*)

Left: Unrealistic moulded ratlines and shrouds which are far too heavy and out of scale.

bands tightly bound around the mast to help strengthen them) in place. The masts have heavily moulded lugs to locate the mast and yards, but these are best removed with the yards pinned in place for an authentic appearance. Like all plastic masts, they are easily pulled out of plumb when rigging. Slender parts like the topgallants and royals are better replaced with tapered wooden dowels for rigidity. The bowsprit is a nicely detailed piece spoiled by a moulded ring to mount the spritsail yard, and the bowsprit's jib is very thin and should be replaced with brass rod.

The standing rigging (deadeyes, shrouds and ratlines) are thick plastic parts mounted to channels glued onto the side of the hull to help the less experienced modeller, but for a scale appearance these items are best replaced with thread equiv-

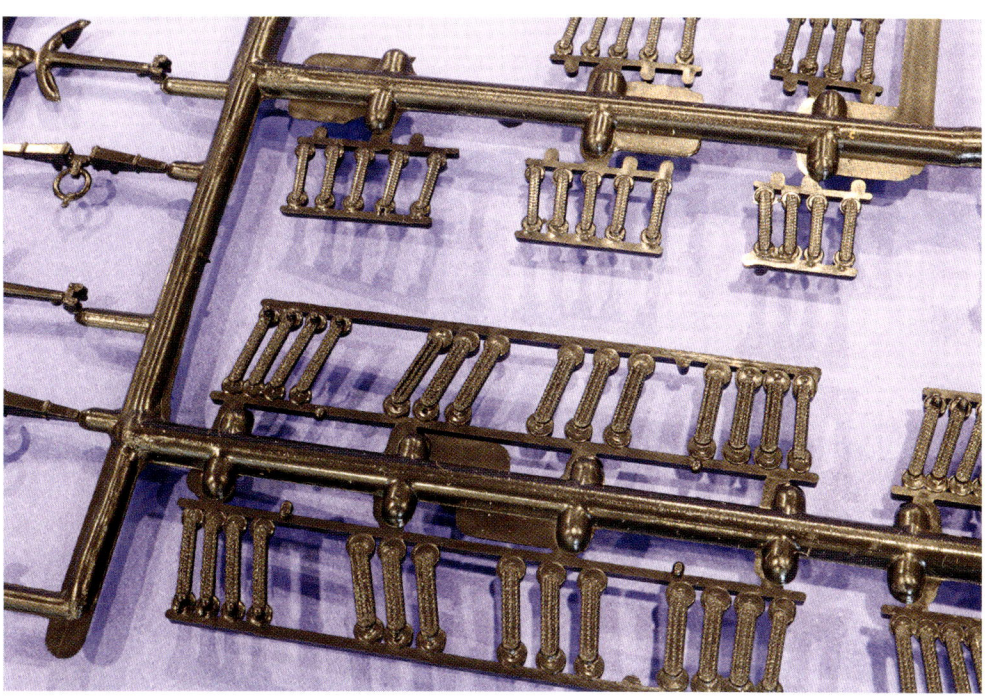

Left: Moulded deadeyes and lanyards.

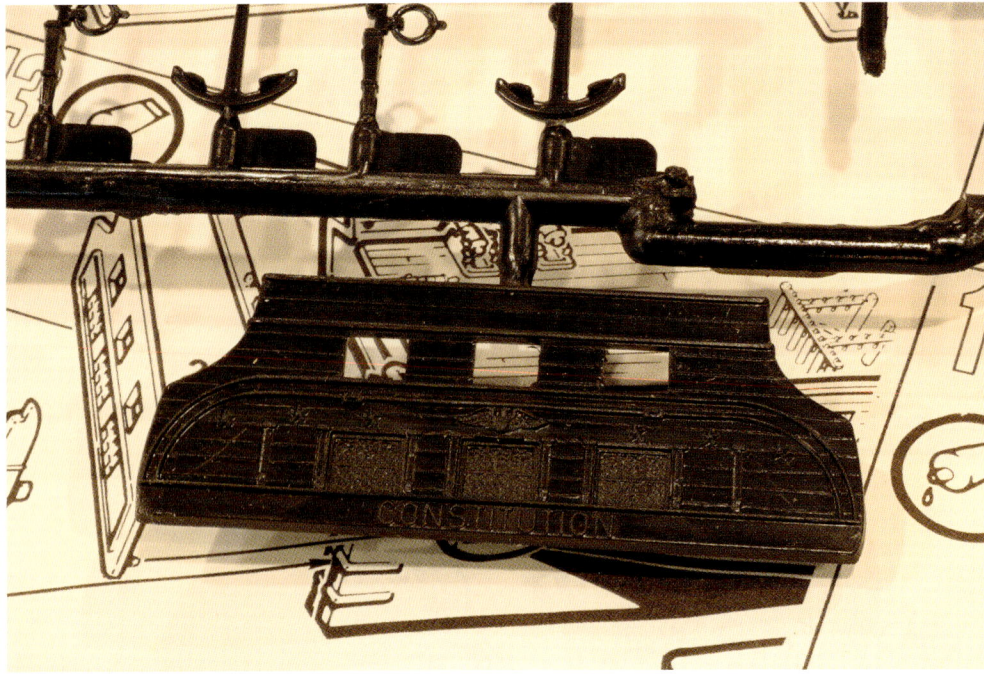

Right: This version of Revell's stern transom was first fitted to the ship in the 1870s and is still present on the vessel today.

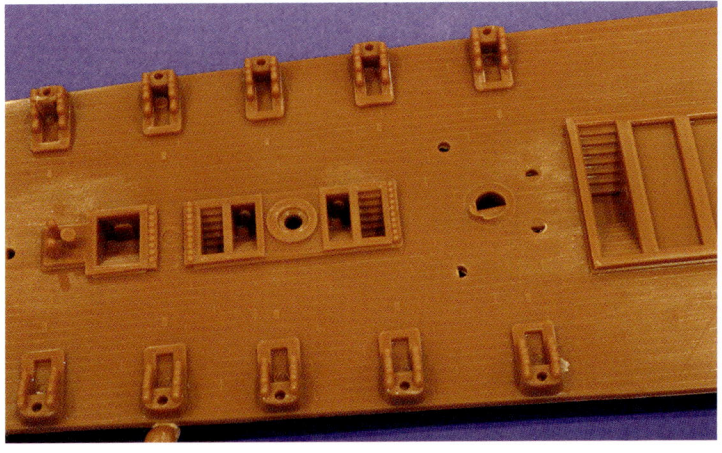

Above: The gun carriages are moulded into the deck and lack detail.

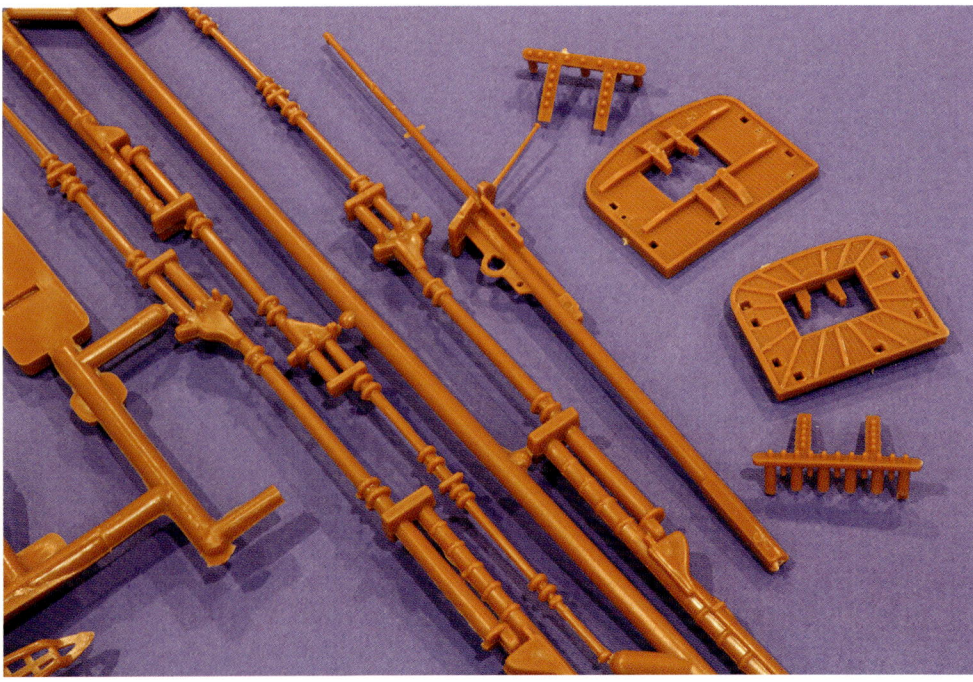

Right: The ship's masts are each moulded as a single part.

alents using miniaturist techniques described in this author's *Sailing Ships from Plastic Kits* (2024). The kit's sails are vacuformed in thin styrene sheet and feature reef lines, seam lines, and a coarse fabric weave texture. They are stiff and take care when *bending* (attaching) them to the yards to hang naturally. The running rigging (lines that are used for raising, lowering, shaping, and controlling the sails and yards) is entirely done with a single thickness of tan thread, and no blocks or other rigging gear provided. Several different weights of thread should be used to represent the different types of ropes and cables used in rigging, and items like blocks can be simulated with tiny discs of punched card painted dark brown. Out of the box, the kit provides the modeller with a detailed model but with some basic refinements it will produce a more convincing impression, albeit from an indeterminate period of the ship's history.

PYRO USS *CONSTITUTION* (Kit #170-69)   1:450 Scale

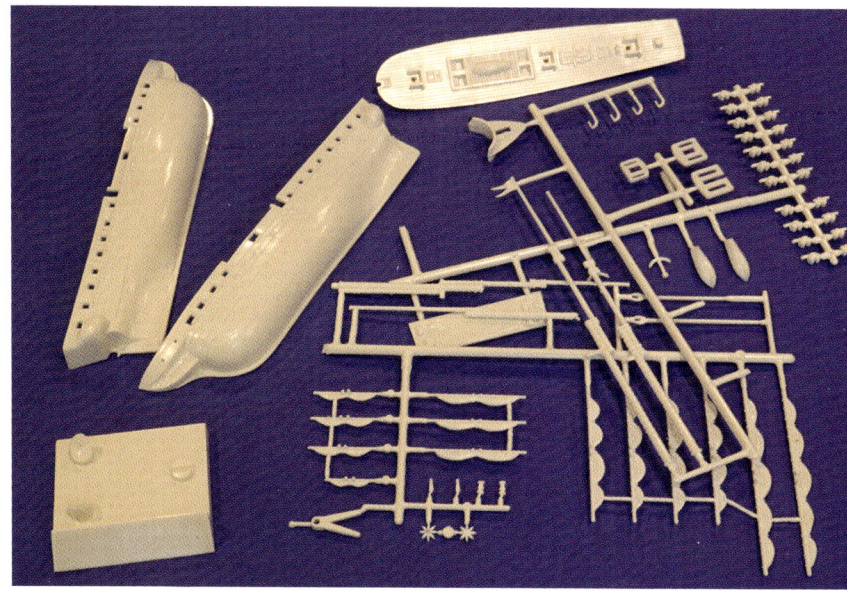

A 1950s vintage kit, the hull profile is recognisable as *Constitution* although the trailboards in the bow are oversized. The hull features planking detail and fine renditions of deadeyes and chainplates, but the underwater hull is devoid of any copper plating. The transom is plain but can be detailed with a paper tracing of the area on to which the lights and decoration are drawn and coloured, cut out, and glued into place. The masts are one-piece mouldings, with separate yards carrying partially furled sails. The deck detailing is neat and in bold relief to aid painting. No pretence at rigging is provided, but the instructions do illustrate a few representative lines. Overall, a neat little model that is very much a product of its time, but worthy of a second look for a serious miniaturist who can invest the time and effort detailing it.

LINDBERGH/ROUND 2 BARBARY PIRATE FELUCCA (Kit #HL205/12)   1:250 Scale

This kit first appeared in 1953 under the Pyro label. The model resembles a large felucca with lateen sails and cannon as seen in contemporary illustrations. This kit features oars that were fitted to some feluccas to out-manoeuvre ships relying solely on wind. The mouldings are heavy but scratch-built refinements will capture the grace and beauty of these vessels. The largest castings are the huge sails that can serve as a pattern for paper replacements. Every North Africa felucca was a 'one off', designed and built by an experienced local shipwright to his own designs rendering any remarks about the kit's accuracy nonsensical. Nevertheless, the felucca typifies the opponents of the US Navy in the Barbary War.

AIRFIX **HMS SHANNON** (Kit #1285)   Unknown Scale

There are no kits of any of *Constitution*'s British adversaries. However, in the small kit world there is *Shannon* which captured *Chesapeake*. The kit was first released in 1954 as a waterline model with a moulded seascape. In 1973 the hull halves were modified to a full hull and a display stand replaced the seascape base. The model is to an indeterminate scale, and the hull profile only very broadly resembles a *Leda* class frigate, with the head of the ship a gross monstrosity with cheeks that are far too heavy and large. The hull sides sport closed gunports, channels, deadeye and chainplate detail. The stern is blank, but a printed paper sheet with the lights and decoration is provided on the instruction sheet to be cutout and pasted in place. The masts are one-piece affairs, to which yards with integrally moulded billowing sails are attached. It is a toylike model but built from the bag and painted on a seascape makes an interesting, if nostalgic, display piece.

BILLING BOATS **USS CONSTITUTION** (Kit #508)
1:100 Scale

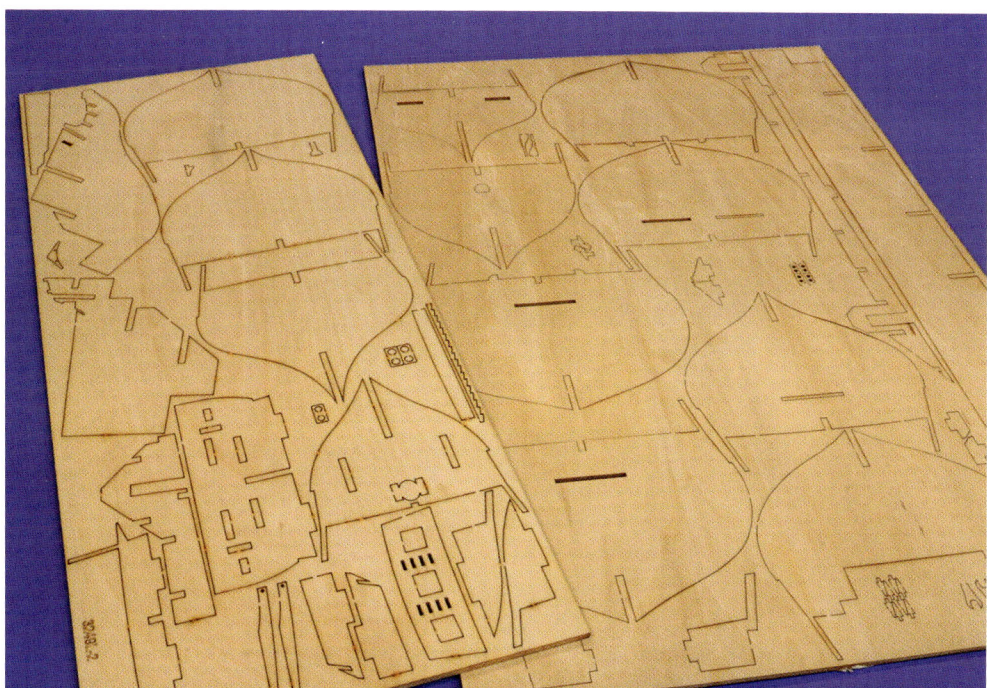

Left: Laser-cut hull bulkheads in quality plywood.

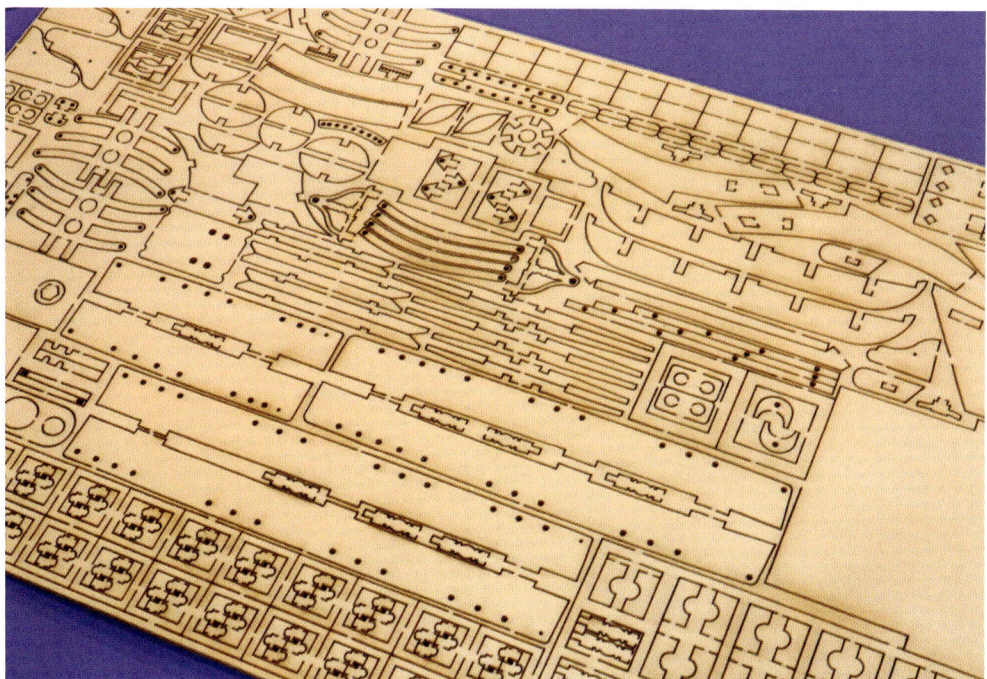

Left: One of the sheets containing hundreds of laser-cut parts.

Billing Boats' wooden kit is aimed at a less experienced wooden kit modeller with several simplifications to ease construction but at the same time it provides the experienced modeller with a solid base to indulge their whims. The kit represents the ship as she now appears in Boston. Construction begins with the slotted false keel to which transverse bulkheads are glued to form the basic framework of the ship's hull. One of most arduous tasks of wooden ship modelling is plotting the gunports on a curved surface. This problem is solved by the two fully shaped plywood laser-cut bulwarks with all the locations for the spar and main deck guns cut out that takes the hull's curve into account. Once in place, the entire skeleton is planked with a single layer of wood that goes over the bulwarks and the lower hull in the conventional manner (planking a hull with wood strips is demonstrated in this author's 2022 *Ship Models from the Age of Sail: Building and Enhancing Commercial Kits*).

The scroll work on the bow and stern decorations are printed card that is cut out and glued to the area. These details are easily made in relief by building them up from artist's gesso and then painted using the printed decorations as a guide. The spar deck is fully fitted out with guns and details, but the main gun deck is not included. The guns that inhabit this deck are represented by dummy barrels that are fixed into holes drilled into the hull sides.

Right: Turned brass gun barrels and a roll of copper wire used to strop deadeyes.

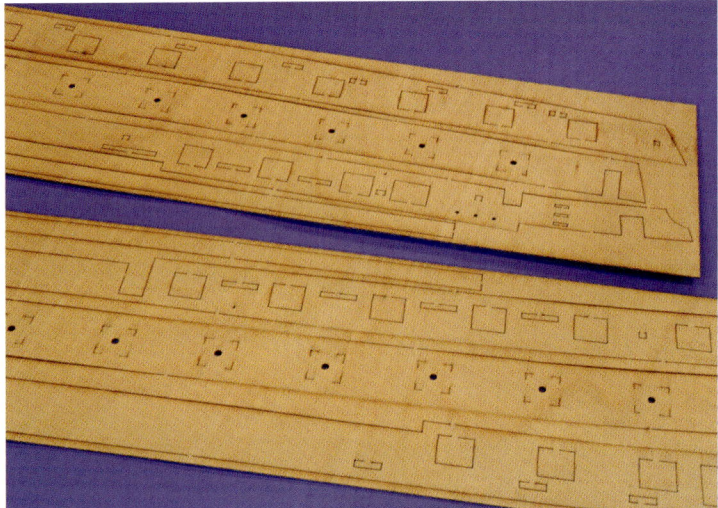

Above: Fully shaped hull bulwarks with gunport and gun locations cut in place. No measuring required.

A view of the main gun deck from the ship's waist is neatly blocked by a set of gratings.

Although the plans show some elements of standing and running rigging, key lines like the braces (lines to control the side-to-side pivot of the yards) are simplified by having the rope ends tied to the end of a spar, omitting the tackle and lines that run down to their belaying points on the hull. In contrast, the halyards and lifts are complete with all the blocks to show the viewer how the yards moved up and down the masts. This mixed approach to rigging does give the novice modeller an authentic rigging experience, but for the more experienced modeller the kit provides the opportunity to rig every line with the additions of extra blocks and line purchased separately.

Right: A selection of the mixed media fittings, including anchors in plastic, belaying pins turned from brass, brown plastic cleats, deadeyes in wood, cast brass ship's wheel, copper eyebolts and pre-cut brass tubes.

Left: A selection of wooden blocks, deadeyes, and copper eyebolts.

Left: Rigging line, hammock netting, soft copper sheet, and printed bow decorations.

To be fair, most experienced modellers, no matter the kit, will supplement those provided in any kit – even replacing them all – with rigging blocks, deadeyes, and line of assorted sizes to replicate the ship's actual rigging.

The kit parts are laser-cut in high-quality plywood. Items like the side gallery lights feature fully cut window frames for a see-through look. The mast tops are built in layers to replicate the non-slip tread floors, and all carronade carriages are assembled from several parts for authenticity. The wood planking strips included are straight, cleanly cut, and free of knots or blemishes. Masts and spars are to be shaped by the modeller from lengths of birch dowel. Some fittings are provided in styrene plastic (*eg*, anchors), but gun barrels are from turned brass. Printed cloth flags, four thickness of white rigging thread (must be dyed black or tan), a roll of fine textured canvas to make sails, fabric tuille for hammock nettings, and brass wire complete the package. The fully illustrated instructions and two large general arrangement plans provide all the essential information to build the model.

No copper plates are provided; instead the bottom of the hull is to be painted copper, with a strip of red lead anti-fouling paint replicating the ship's present appearance. The Billing kit, given its affordable price provides the means to build a presentable replica of the present-day *Constitution* out of the box, but is a rich canvas for an experienced modeller to create a highly detailed model with scratch-built and after-market accessories.

BLUEJACKET USS *CONSTITUTION* 1812–1815
(Kit #1018)   1:96 Scale

■ This kit embodies a more traditional approach to wooden kits with its partially carved wooden hull and an extensive reliance on finely cast pewter parts (a form of lead-free metal often referred to as 'Britannia Metal') for the ship's rigging and details. The finished model is a representation the ship during the War of 1812 from research by Mr Laurence Arnot. Every detail of her appearance was thoroughly researched, and sources documented in the hefty instruction booklet that also provides an unprecedented amount of instruction on how to build the model. Everything is covered – from how to carve the wooden hull down to its final shape, finishing wood, how to strop deadeyes and blocks, and tying knots for the ratlines. Four full size plans illustrate the locations of hull details, sails, and rigging. The rigging plan specifies the type of blocks to use, the correct gauge of line, and which belaying pin or bitt the line is attached to. The plans and instruction booklet are available separately for the modeller to convert any other plastic or wooden kit to her appearance in late 1812.

The centrepieces of the kit is a machine-carved wooden hull up to the main gun deck with thick bulwarks that enclose the spar deck. Once the hull is worked down to its final shape and bulwarks thinned, the keel, stem and sternposts are cut from thick sheet following the plans and attached to the hull. Because the hull is solid wood, there is no see-through effect on the stern and quarter gallery lights. The effect can be simulated by drilling out deep holes to hollow out the galleries in these locations. The gunports will have to be plotted from the plans and cut out. The hull is not meant to be planked but just painted once complete. However, Bluejacket offer a set of thin basswood strips to plank over the

Right: The rough-cut solid wooden hull to be refined by the modeller. The shape is only approximate and some considerable carving and sanding is required to take the block down to the hull lines.

Far right: The ship's launch is also pre-carved wood. The remaining boats are cast is pewter.

Right: A selection of the etched brass parts that includes gratings, hammock cranes, and chainplates, and the ship's stove. A fully detailed ship's transom includes windows and relief-etched decoration. The transom design where 'drops' replaced the pillars between the lights is from late 1812 and can be seen in paintings of the battle with *Java*.

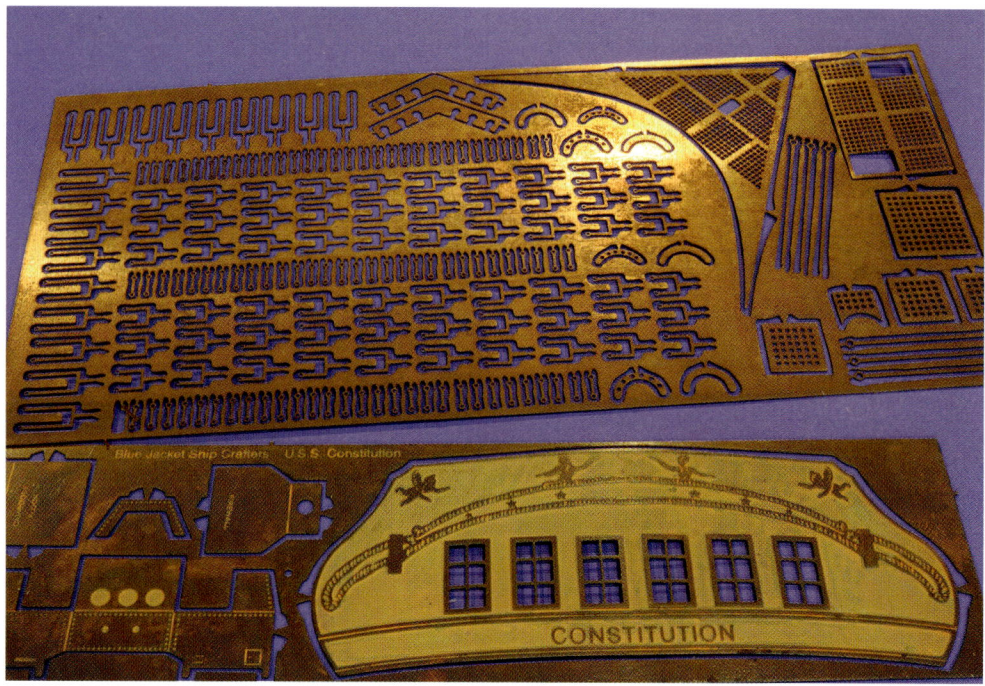

hull if desired. Unfortunately, no copper plate is provided for the underwater hull, instead relying on paint which just does not look right on a model of this scale and detail. Self-adhesive copper foil cut into scale plates is a better option, or Bluejacket's own, if rather expensive, etched-copper plates complete with accurate nail head detail can be used.

The main and spar decks are provided as scribed basswood sheet. These are cut into lengthwise halves to fit inside the hull. It is an uncomplicated way of laying a simple deck, but it will be very difficult to fit waterways and nib the plank ends into them for complete authenticity. Moreover, because the deck planks are scribed as single continuous grooves along the length of the sheet, plank butts and *trennals* (wooden pegs used to fasten the planks to the deck beams) must be drawn in with a sharp pencil. Care must be taken with these thin scribed sheets of wood. Any contact with moisture will make them curl beyond use, so keep them dry and use epoxy, cellulose or impact (contact) cement to glue them down to the hull. Bluejacket also offer sheets of deck planking material made up of strips of wood glued together with black glue.

Over 2000 pewter fittings cover decoration, guns, carriages, boats, companionways, wheels, capstans; blocks comprise single, double, treble and jeer types, and the deadeyes are complete with scores with some provided as ready stropped. The reason for using these cast metal blocks is because they look exactly like real blocks. Thirty years ago, kit-supplied blocks were unrealistic rectangles of wood with a hole, so Bluejacket introduced an extensive line of cast pewter blocks that had the correct shape and details (*eg*, sheaves and scores) to fill the need. They are well cast but all will need some clean-up of flash, and the cast holes need to be opened with a fine drill bit. Painting them is easily accomplished by stringing them on a piece of wire, priming and painting them with an airbrush. At the present time, it is fair to say that these cast blocks are on the verge of becoming obsolete. Highly authentic blocks with the same details are now available milled from fine hardwoods, or 3D printed coloured resin.

Two sheets of etched brass provide the hammock cranes and fittings, including bow gratings and the transom. No cloth for sails is provided but a full-size sail plan is included. Masts and yards are shaped from birch dowel. Items like the mast caps and *boots* (covers that surround the base of the mast to prevent the ingress of water) are provided as pewter castings. In keeping with Bluejacket's quest for authenticity, twenty spools of thread are provided to replicate the different sizes of rope used in real rigging. Eight spools are in black for the standing rigging, and twelve in white/tan for the running rigging in high-quality thread. The remaining fittings include mesh for the hammocks, a correct 15-star US flag and ensigns. No display options are provided so a plinth and pedestals will have to be supplied by yourself. In summary, a well-researched and presented kit that provides the modeller interesting modelmaking challenges. The kit is the most expensive on the market today, and if you add the optional hull and planking sets, coppering, and display items, it will double your already not inconsiderable investment.

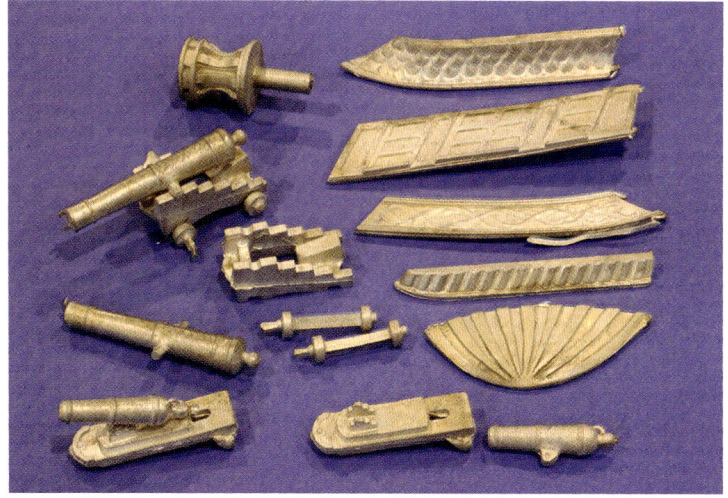

Above: Side gallery decorations, guns and carriages, and capstan are fine cast pewter.

Left: Ship's boats and stern decorations are cast in pewter. The Bluejacket kit does not provide a full suite of ship's boats and extras must be purchased separately for a full complement.

Left: A selection of the hundreds of pewter rigging blocks and deadeyes. They are very realistic but will take some work to clean up before painting.

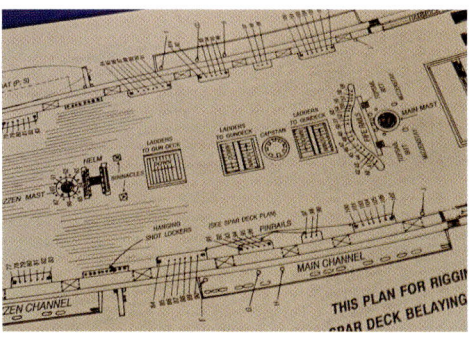

Left: The belaying plan.

MODEL SHIPWAYS **USS CONSTITUTION** (Kit #2040)
1:76.8 or 5/32in = 1ft Scale

This is a single plank on bulkhead kit designed by the noted modeller Mr Ben Lankford representing the ship after her 1996 restoration. The kit was designed using plans and photographs from her 1927 restoration, but the details are for her

Right: The ship's boats are built up 'bread and butter style', where the layers are glued together and then smoothed off inside and out to form a perfect boat.

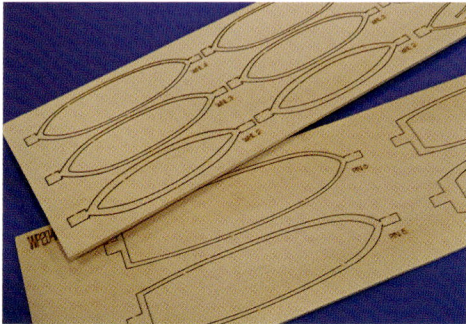
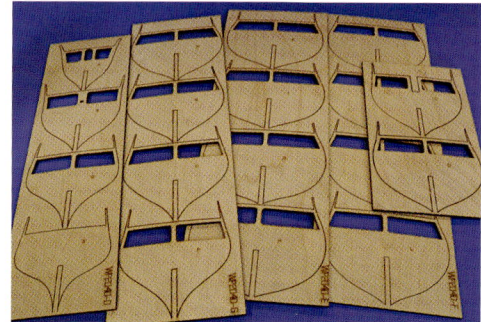

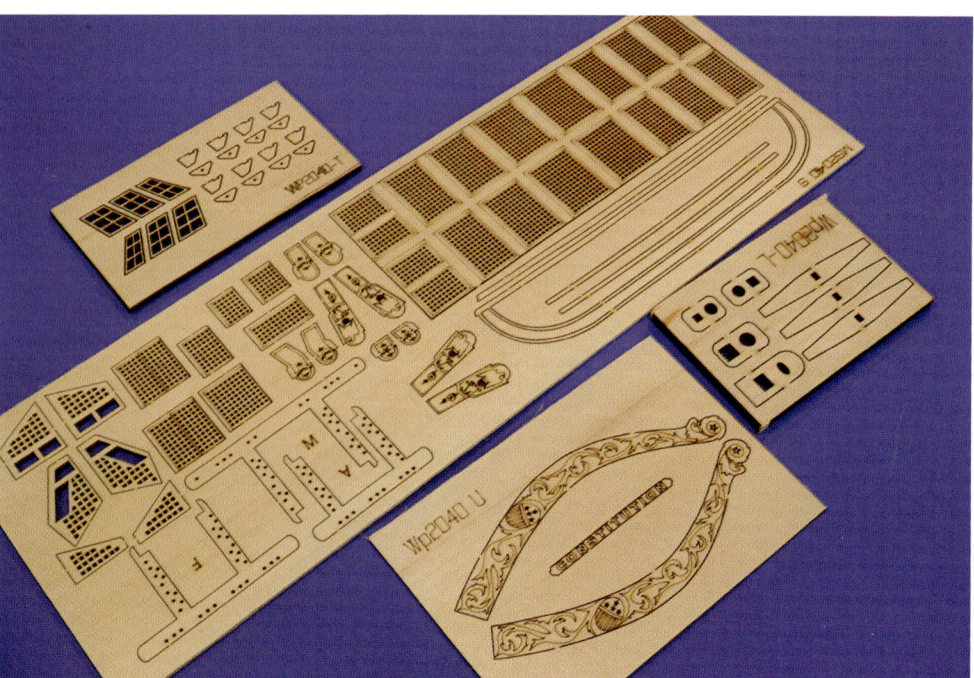

present appearance, taken from the museum ship in Boston. In this kit you will find parts for contemporary items like the round berth deck scuttles, and the plans include details of the awnings that shade tourists from the sun, and the fenders fitted to the hull sides to prevent chafing against her moorings. However, the kit provides an excellent basis to build the ship at any period during her history.

The kit is laser-cut throughout with the bulkheads, false keel, keel, stem and sternposts from high quality ply. A feature of the kit is that the close spacing of the bulkheads prevents the hull planking from sagging between them. The bulkheads have beams cut into them for the main and spar deck, but the kit design closes off the main gun deck with the guns themselves represented by dummy gun barrels. Views of the gun deck from the spar deck are blocked with finely cut gratings. However, should the modeller wish to fully detail the main gun deck, a false deck from thin ply can be cut to fit and glued to the beams then planked. The modeller Tom Stazione (see page 50) took advantage of this design feature to build a fully detailed lower gun deck as the ship would have appeared in 1812. This is the thoughtful manner in which the kit was designed; out-of-the-box it builds one way, but part design allows the modeller several alternative options that are highlighted throughout the well written and easily followed instruction booklet. Lankford has designed several kits for Model Shipways, and the ones this author has built came out superb using only what was in the box.

High-quality basswood is provided for the hull and deck planking, all being straight and clear. Birch and walnut dowel are used for the masts and yards. Laser cut parts provide the caps and fighting tops. In this kit, the spar deck is planked with individual strips of wood that allows for fitting a waterway and for each plank to be properly joggled into place as shown on the exceptionally detailed plans, along with the shift of the butts and trennalling patterns. The ships' fittings are a mix of cleanly cast white metal and etched brass. The ship's decoration like the sculpted eagle and pilasters are cast in white metal, but the scroll work on the cutwater is laser etched into the wood for the modeller to paint in or build up from artist's gesso.

The beautifully detailed plans provide full rigging details, and should you wish to add sails, these are drawn out in detail. The deadeyes are turned walnut with wire provided to strop them. The wooden rigging blocks are generic items whose appearance can be improved by sanding them to be a little more oval shaped. Six diameters of black and tan rigging thread are provided to recreate the different sizes used on the real ship. In summary, the design of the model and the extensive supporting instructions and drawings allow the modeller a lot of choice in how to build the model. With some research and rudimentary scratch-building skills you can build an authentic model of *Constitution* at any time in her career. Coupled with the excellent quality of all the kit's contents and instructions, the affordable price represents excellent value. Model Shipways also offer a cut-away version of the ship made to the same high-quality standards as the full hull model. An excellent build by Tom Cutherbertson is shown on pages 48-49.

Above: Just a small selection of the extensive white metal castings providing all the fittings and guns.

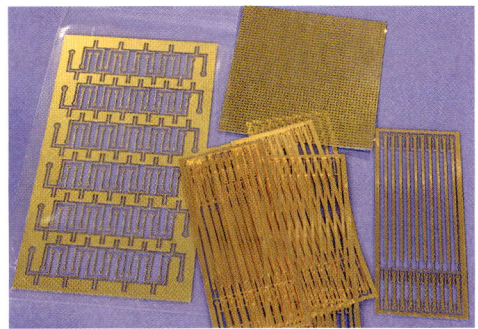

Left: Etched brass provides the hammock cranes, gratings, and chainplate details.

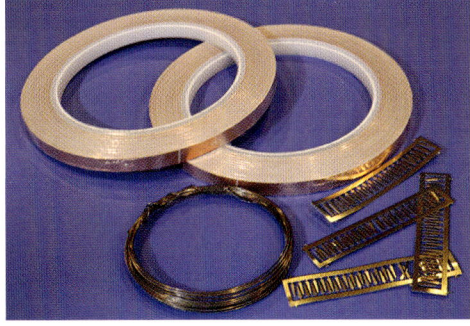

Left: Rolls of self-adhesive copper tape for the underwater sheathing, and copper and brass wire stock to fashion items like deadeye strops in different sizes are provided.

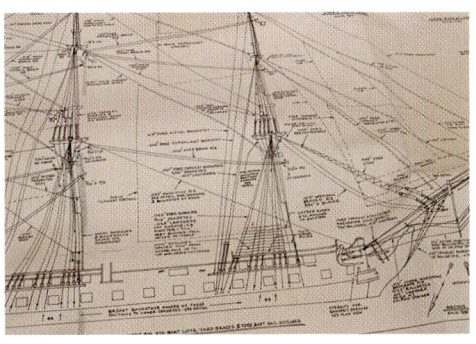

Left: A sample of Ben Lankford's superb plans to build a model of the ship.

REVELL *USS CONSTITUTION* 'OLD IRONSIDES'
(Kit #85-0938) 1:96 Scale

This large-scale kit from 1965 is a remarkable example of design from the heyday of plastic kits. The hull moulding features delicate decorative works at the bow, fine planking detail and a fully detailed copper hull where each scale plate is covered with scale rivets. A realistic woodgrain texture is applied to the exterior and interior of the hull that will either delight or annoy modellers. The quarter galleries are beautifully moulded with decorative work, and the lights are hollow with finely moulded mullions and frames to be glazed with clear acetate. Revell has made some effort to show *Constitution*'s 1812 appearance with the stern and transom decoration but all else is consistent with the 1927 restoration.

The gun and spar decks are moulded with raised deck planking detail with a wood grain finish. A waterway is moulded in place, but the deck planks are not properly nibbed into them. No butt or trennal detail is included but can be scribed into the plastic. The deck fittings include pin rails, bitts, wheels, and pumps all displaying scale delicacy. The detailed masts and yards are moulded in two halves, allowing a length of brass rod (supplied yourself) to be glued into them before joining the halves together to provide strength under the

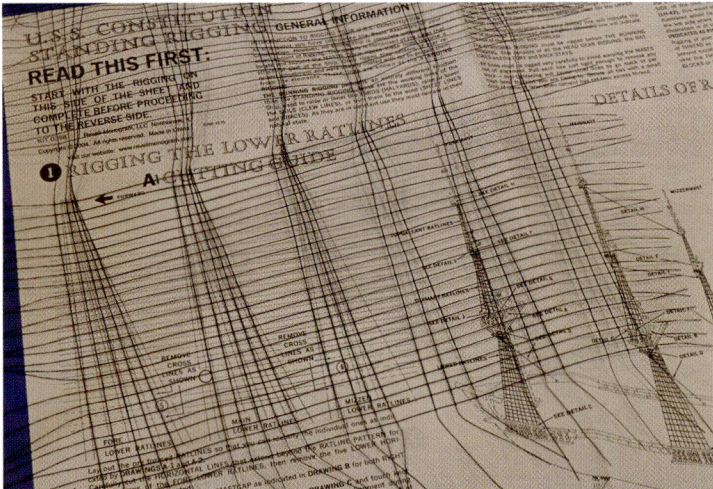

Above: Unrealistic rubber coated thread is provided for the shrouds and ratlines.

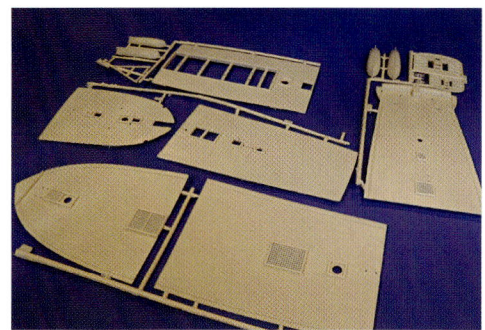

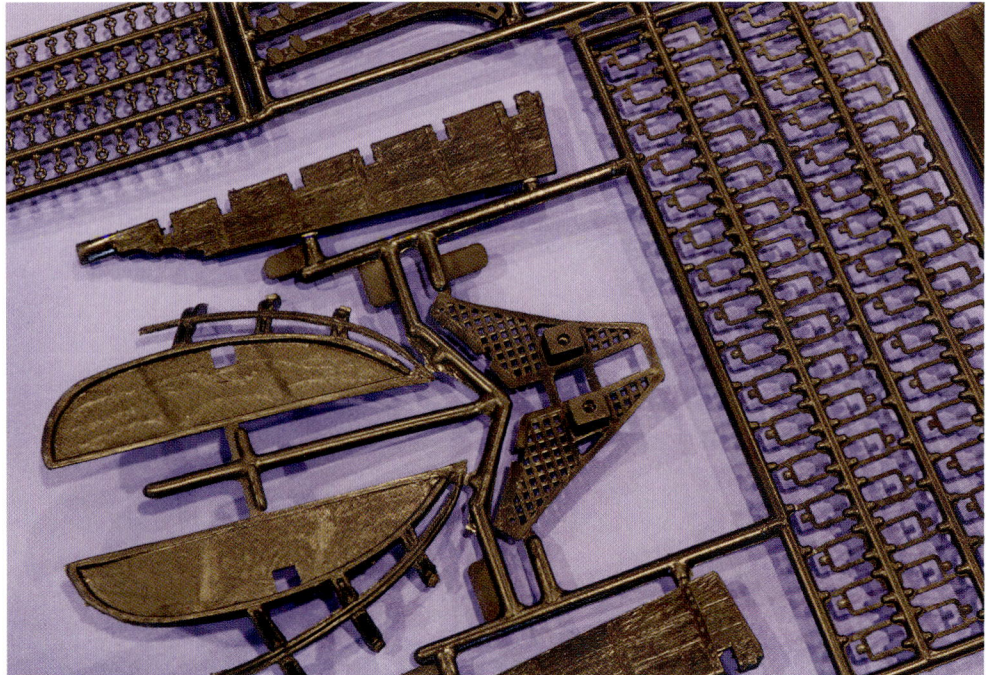

Right: Forecastle parts showing boarded up cheeks.

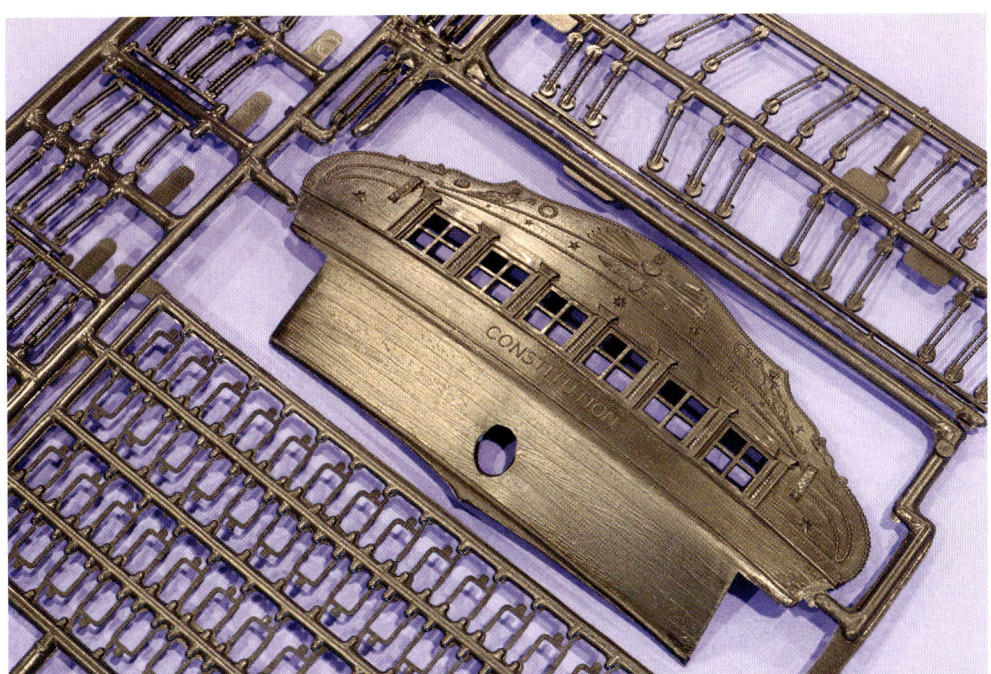

Left: Stern transom that is very similar to the 1812 model built by Isaac Hull's crew.

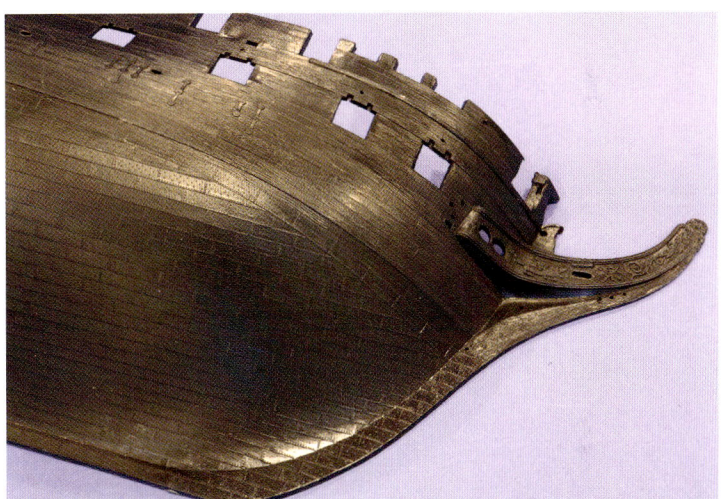

strain of rigging. Like most plastic kits, the standing rigging's deadeyes and lanyards are moulded as a single plastic part. However, clever design work went into these parts with the deadeyes being moulded in halves with a different pattern of lanyards moulded into them. When glued together it yields a convincing impression that the lanyards have been properly *reeved* (laced) in the correct order. The deadeye assemblies are ready stropped and moulded into the channels that fixes them to the hull. Separately moulded chainplates and chains secure the shrouds to the hull.

Interestingly, the shrouds and ratlines are provided as rubber coated thread weavings. The weavings are cut out using a template and the lower portion is fixed to the back of the deadeyes and the upper end fixed to the top of the mast. The problem is that the gauge of the threads used for the shrouds are identical for ratlines and do not represent the heavy cables required to hold the masts in place. In this large scale, all the standing rigging should be prototypical using scale deadeyes, reeving them properly, with the modeller learning to tie knots for the ratlines.

The kit's running rigging is set up like the real ship with detailed instructions on where to fix blocks, run the thread and belay it in the proper place. The modeller's job is made easier by the provision of ready stropped blocks moulded in brown plastic with a *becket* (ring) to tie the rigging thread. Several

Above: Ready moulded blocks fully stropped complete with becket.

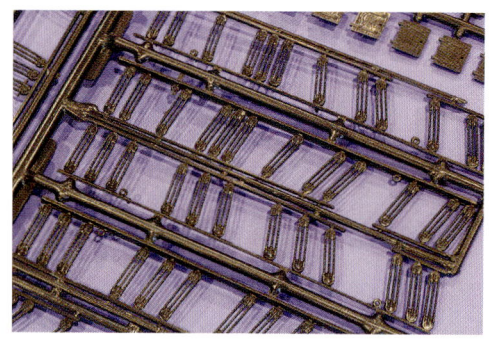

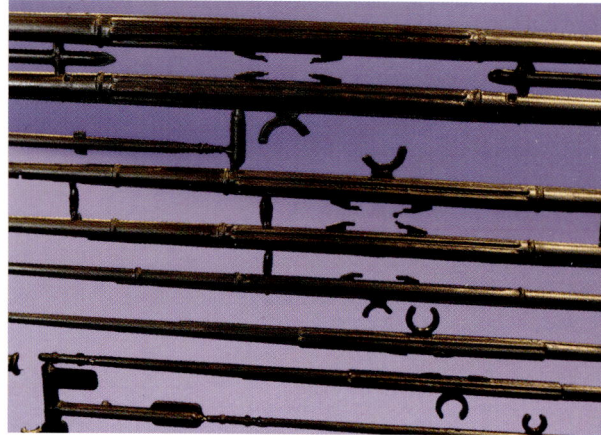

Above, right: Well moulded deadeyes and lanyards to simplify rigging.

Right: Yards are moulded with unrealistic lugs to aid attachment to the masts. They should be removed, and the yards pinned in place.

sizes of single, double, and triple blocks are provided. Revell's rigging plan is simplified but all the major lines are present for a satisfying overall appearance. The sails are vacuformed in a light tan plastic displaying plenty of detail, but in this large scale, real cloth sails cannot be bettered. The painting instructions have the ship painted in the well-known black hull with white stripe scheme from her 1927 restoration.

MAMOLI **USS *CONSTITUTION*** (Kit #MV31) 1:93 Scale

Forty years ago, Luigi Volonte founded Mamoli as one of first wooden ship kit producers in the world. In 2016 Daniel Dûsek took over the line and introduced modern materials and laser cutting to replace the printed, hand- or die-cut parts of the original kits. Happily, despite the upgrade of the kit line, they remained faithful to Volonte's designs that have a special élan that reflects the look and feel of the hand-hewn nature of sailing ships. This is first noticed on the artistically hand-drawn full-size plans supplemented by charming inset drawings showing the modeller how to do things. Tasks like cutting and filing out gunports, how to tie lines, or bevelling planks are illustrated. The fully illustrated drawings are supported with short descriptions in multiple languages.

The kit's hull is double plank on bulkhead design. After sheathing the framework in the first layer of planks, the gunports must be plotted from the plans, cut out, and framed in. This first layer gives the modeller a base to get the hull shape exactly right. The second layer of planks is the finish wood, and the kit provides thin strips of walnut that can be painted or

Left: A sample of Luigi Volonte's beautifully drawn plans.

stained as desired. The kit's wood strips are straight, free of knots and respond well to the application of heat or water to soften the wood for bending. The main gun deck is closed from view and the guns are muzzle-ends set into recesses in the hull. The spar deck is planked with strips of wood over a thin plywood subdeck, and fully fitted with guns, bitts, capstans and boats. This method of laying the deck allows a waterway to be laid, and the planks to be properly nibbed into them. Belaying pin racks are cut from strip wood to be filled with turned wood pins. The kit was designed at a time when research materials were difficult to obtain in Italy, and the one area Volonte guessed at is the stern transom. His design shows two tiers of three lights, more characteristic of a European galleon than a workman-like American frigate. For modeller's desiring accuracy, the transom can be easily rebuilt from thin ply with the proper six light configuration. The *Constitution* and her sisters did not carry much in the way of decoration, so scratch-building these parts is no hardship.

The masts and yards are shaped from birch and walnut dowels, and the plans illustrate the rigging in detail. Generic wooden blocks and turned hardwood deadeyes are provided. Several spools and hanks

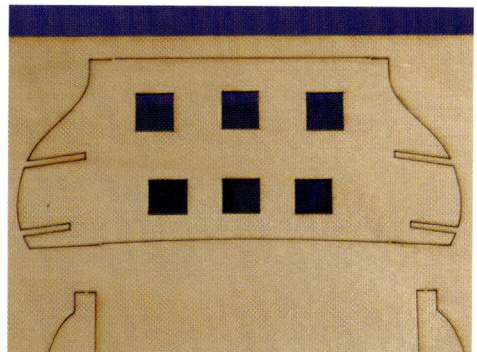

Left: The fanciful stern transom that can be remade from thin ply with the correct window configuration if desired.

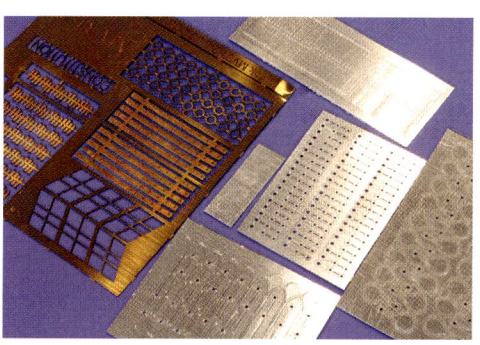

Left: Hull bulkheads and false keel are cut from quality plywood.

Above: A small selection of the wooden blocks and deadeyes, flags, rigging line and of the smaller fittings in white metal.

Above, right: The cast white metal parts are well detailed.

of thread supply the rigging. Etched parts in steel and brass provide deadeye strops and chainplates. The ship's bow decoration comes in the form of hefty white metal castings. Stern decoration is minimal, with a laser-cut and etched bald eagle from thin ply. The ship's boats and davits are white metal and are to be detailed with wood strip.

For any modeller looking back fondly on the kit designs of his youth, this kit is ideal. Nostalgia is not something to scoff at – just look at how many plastic modellers eagerly snap up re-released 1960s vintage Airfix plastic kits in a yearning for a bygone time. However, with some research, a very authentic model can be built from the quality materials in the box.

MAMOLI USS *CONSTITUTION* CROSS-SECTION (Kit #MV32) 1:93 Scale

Right: All of the kit's major components are neatly laser-cut in a variety of quality wood stock.

An ideal companion to the Mamoli model is the cross-section model showing a slice of the ship at the mainmast. The decks and hull frames are laser-cut in quality plywood. The interior is filled with guns, pumps and many wooden barrels. About the only thing the modeller will need to add is some scale shale or gravel for the ship's ballast. Following Volonté's drawings, a pleasing model of the ship's interior can be built out of the box. With a little extra effort, for example, scribing scarf joints into the frame faces, making waterways in the bilge and decks from strip, and knees to support the deck will create a more authentic model. Items like below deck

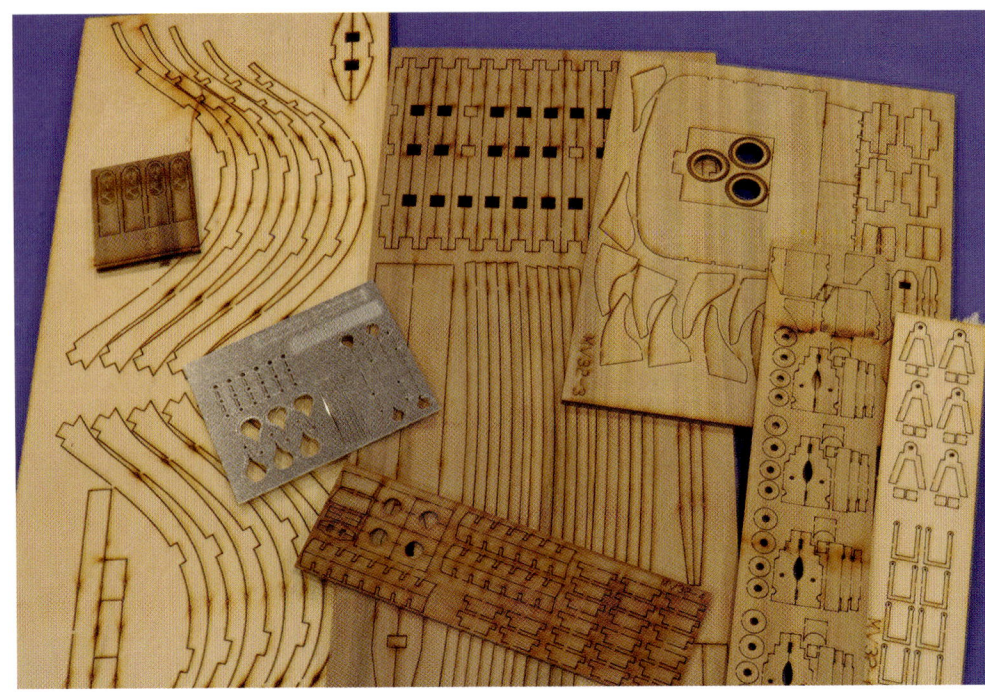

lanterns can be made from dowel and why not add a figure or two? There are plenty of TT scale figures available from model railway shops that can be converted, or 15mm wargame figures would be close in scale to the kit. The kit materials are again excellent quality. A wooden base and laser-etched wooden name plate is included. Combining the full hull model and this cross section would make an extremely eye-catching display.

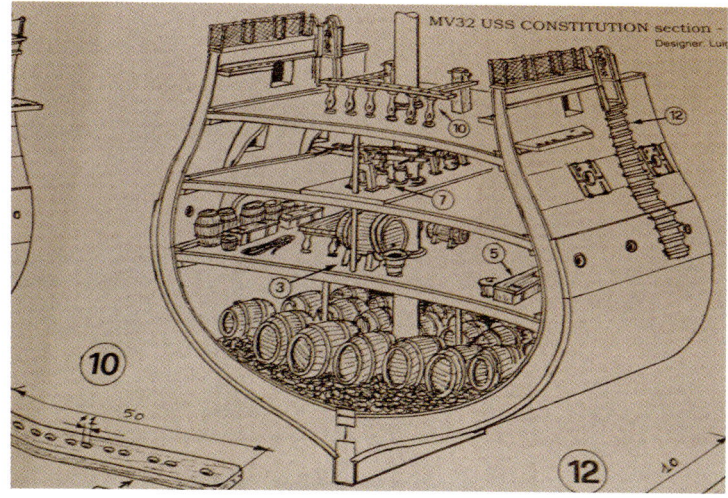

LANGTON USS *CONSTITUTION* (Kit # NA1/2)
1:1200 Scale

Langton Miniatures offers two beautifully cast metal miniatures of *Constitution* with gunports closed (NA1) or 'at quarters' (NA2) with all guns run out. The cast details are proud enough to be easily painted, but not so heavy to make the model look chunky. The model's outline is instantly recognisable as *Constitution* and can also be used for either of her sisters *United States* or *President* in this scale. Available separately are mast and yards cast in white metal, and sail sets in etched brass. The sail sets are generic in that they can be used on any nation's ship with the difference being the size of a ship (*eg*, First Rate, Third Rate, *etc*), and the set of the sail. The modeller and wargamer has a choice of sails to fit ranging from all plain sail to harbour stow with any combination in between. Good luck with the rigging in this tiny scale. I claim my models are rigged with 'invisible thread' that is so fine you cannot see it. There are several wargame

websites that illustrate the many ways these tiny models can be rigged so you can choose the method and materials best suited to you.

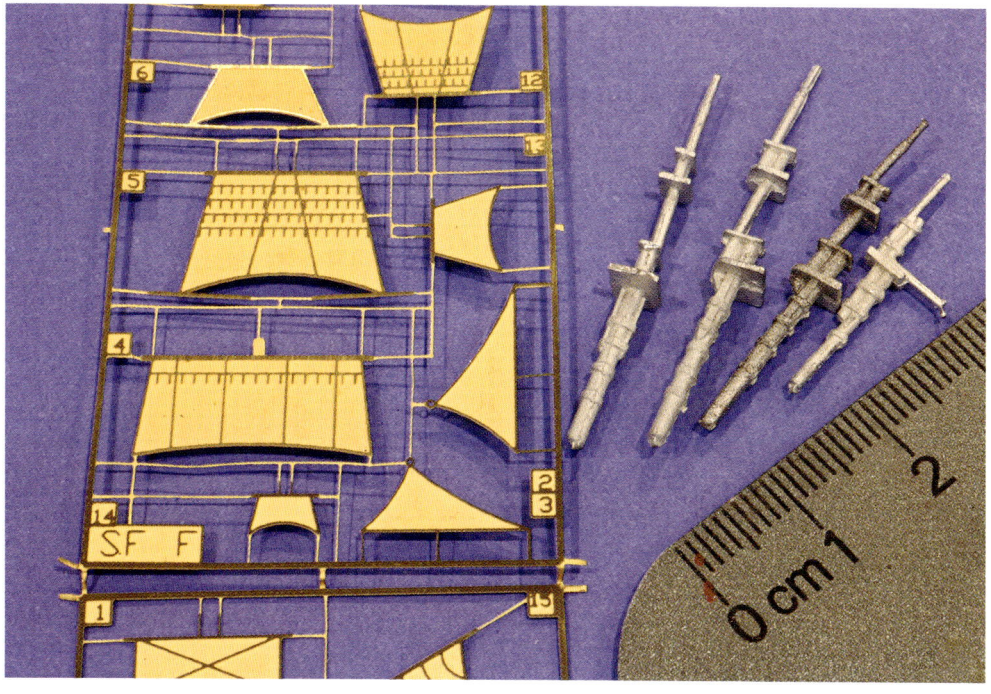

Accessories

HiSMODEL USS *CONSTITUTION* — Various Scales

HiSModel has singled out *Constitution* for an extensive set of accessories that include accurate turned brass guns with wooden carriages, laser-cut and etched wooden decks in two choices of wood, CNC-cut and sewn sails, rigging sets (with downloadable detailed instructions) with authentic wooden blocks for every line carried by the ship, and resin cast stern transom with etched brass light frames. The choice of accessories for this ship vast and readily used with wooden or plastic kits. If you do not see something you need, a quick email to this company will let you know what is possible. Superbly made and researched, their parts are essential to elevating your model to the highest level of detail.

Below: A full suite of sails cut and sewn by CNC in very fine weave cloth. The sails can be dyed an off-white or tan if desired.

Right: A fully detailed resin cast transom that shows the 1812 appearance illustrated by Heinz Karl Marquardt (2005) and taken from a Cornè painting.

Right: HiSModel accessories really brings the plastic kit to new levels of authenticity.

Left and above: The Revell 1:96 kit fitted out with several HiSModel accessories. This superb model was built by Marko Preloznik from the Czech Republic.

MODEL MONKEY USS *CONSTITUTION* — 1:96 Scale

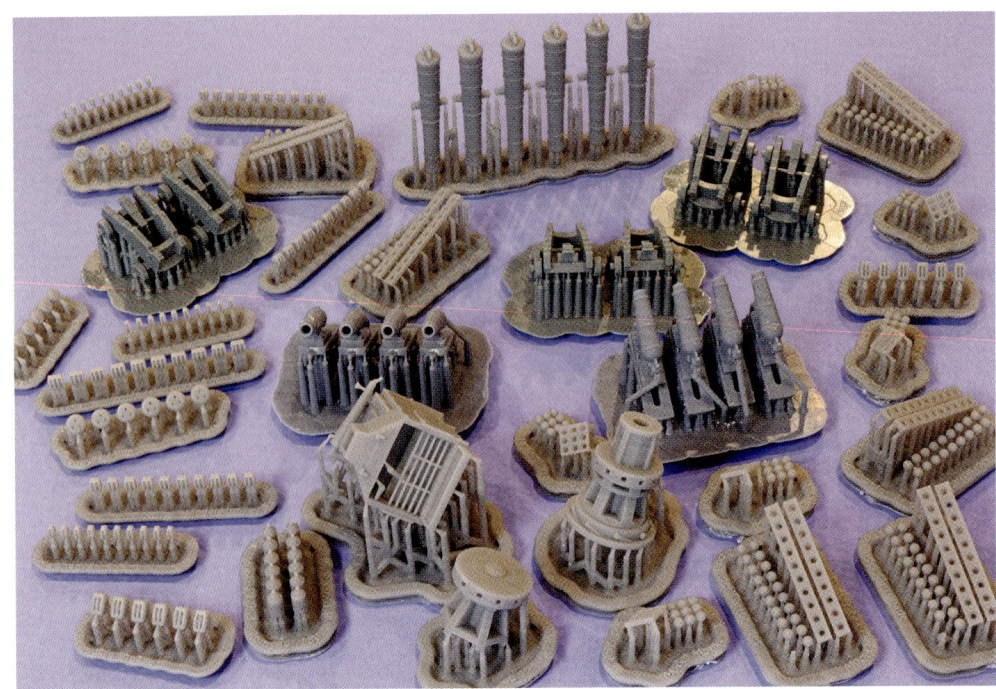

Right: Although the parts were designed for *Constitution*, they are suitable for any sailing warship. The blocks are highly realistic and take a minimum of cleanup before painting.

Above: Stove and capstan. These parts can also be used for any sailing warship in this scale.

Items missing or details lacking from Revell's 1:96 kit are now available as exquisitely designed and 3D printed parts. Lanterns, shot racks, balls, gun carriages, carronade and long gun barrels, capstans, and ship's stove are among the offerings. Model Monkey has also produced a range of perfectly formed blocks in multiple types and sizes suitable for use on any ship. The parts require minimal clean up and the care taken in the printing means that these parts show no print lines: just a coat of paint and you are ready to rig. A superlative line of parts that we hope will only expand in future.

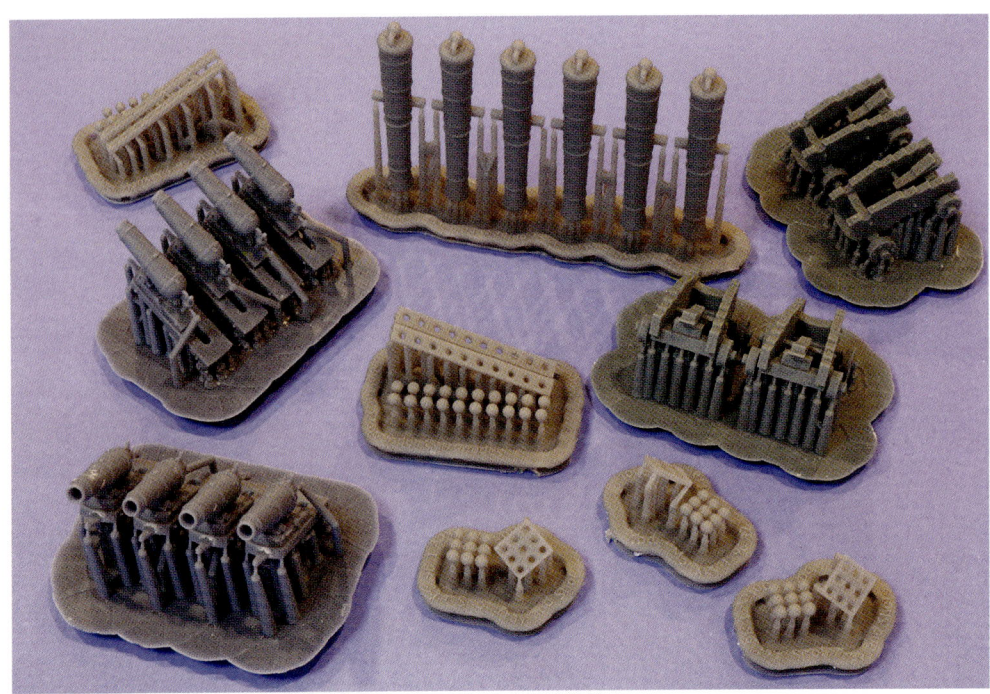

Right: Guns, carronades and shot racks created specifically for the Revell kit.

Modelmakers' Showcase

REVELL USS *CONSTITUTION* 1:96 scale — By EVAN GALE

Mr Gale from southern California has had a long-standing passion for *Constitution*. Shown are some major modifications to the large scale Revell kit to reflect the ship's 1812 appearance. This work is designed to highlight the unique features of the ship, such as cutting away part of the hull to show the ship's (in)famously large frames, and rebuilding the decks to show authentic planking detail. Mr Gale is a member of the Nautical Research Guild and progress on his model is well documented online at www.modelshipworld.com under the screen name FORCE9.

Above: A strake of planking has been omitted and false frames fitted to provide a cut-away view of the ship's hull timbers made from thick styrene.

Above: A new lower gundeck was built from scratch. The strengthening timbers of Humphrey's design that run alongside the main hatch, and the pillars to transfer the weight of the spar deck are recreated. The stove is a Model Monkey 3D printed part.

Left: The hull has received some paint. The painting of the copper is very effective using different shades of copper paint for each square.

MODEL SHIPWAYS **USS *CONSTITUTION*** CROSS-SECTION 1:76.8 scale

By TOM CUTHBERTSON

Mr Culbertson hails from Spokane, Washington and has been an avid modeller since starting with solid wood hull models built when he was in secondary school. The Model Shipways' cross-section of the present-day ship took him two years to build. Uniquely, he used Google Maps' Street View that allowed him to virtually explore the interior and exterior of the ship. The kit was modified to cut away about half of the top deck to yield a clearer view of the cannon and lower deck details.

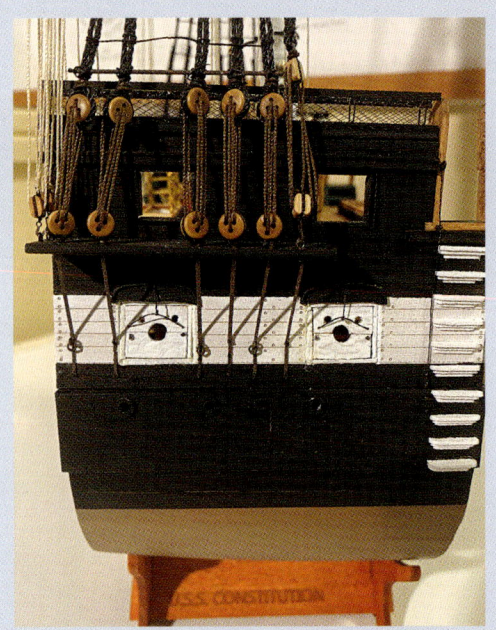

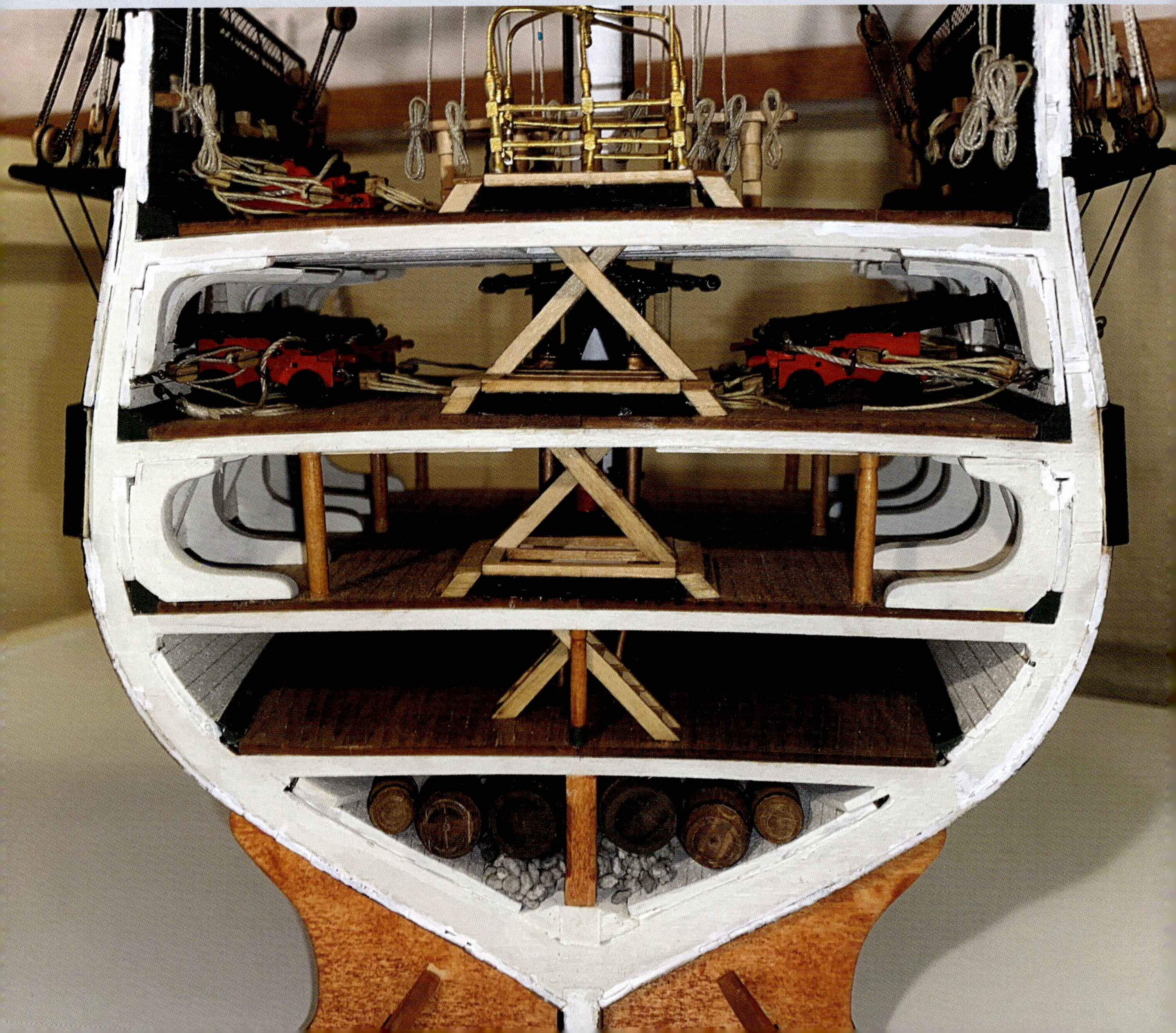

MODELMAKERS' SHOWCASE 49

MODEL SHIPWAYS *USS CONSTITUTION* 1:76.8 scale   By TOM STAZIONE

Mr Stazione lives in the Lakes Region of New Hampshire and has taken advantage of the flexibility designed into the Model Shipways kit to represent the ship during the War of 1812. Tom started the model in 2014 and finished in 2018 and his *Constitution* is a superb example of what can be made from the Model Shipways kit.

Right: View of the scratch-built main gundeck fitted to the Model Shipways kit.

MODELMAKERS' SHOWCASE 51

IMAI **USS *CONSTITUTION*** 1:80 scale   By KATSUJI TSUCHIYA

Mr Tsuchiya lives in Shizuoka, Japan. He has been building wooden sailing ships models from scratch for over 35 years, many that now grace boardrooms and public displays across Japan. The widow of a fellow modeller who started Imai's wooden kit asked Mr Tsuchiya to finish the model. He spent over 11,000 hours refining the kit parts and scratch-building accurate replacements, and all the rigging lines were made on a homemade ropewalk. Mr Tsuchiya is a member of the The Rope modelling club in Tokyo.

REVELL USS *CONSTITUTION* 1:96 scale

By VICTOR YANCOVITCH

Mr Yancovitch from Burns Lake, British Columbia is best known for his magnificent scratch-built wooden ships but took a break and decided on an out-of-the-box build of the Revell kit. However, not satisfied with the kit parts, he fitted HiSModel's new wooden deck, rigging blocks and CNC-cut and sewn sails. The straightforward addition of some after-market accessories elevates what is included in the kit to new levels of realism.

REVELL **USS CONSTITUTION** 1/150 scale   By NORIO URIU

Mr Uriu lives in Ayase-city, Kanagawa, Japan and his unique model is a partly scratch-built half model based on the Revell plastic kit. The kit's plastic hull was sanded smooth and planked over with 0.5mm hinoki cypress strips and 0.2mm thick brass strips below the waterline. The kit was obtained for about $5.00 at a club flea market years ago and after seeing another club member use this technique decided to have a go, taking 18 months of spare time. Mr Uriu has been building large scale sailing ships from scratch for over 40 years. He is a member of the The Rope Tokyo modelling club whose website is in English and Japanese.

Appearance

There are hundreds of illustrations of *Constitution* extant, but only a few are contemporary with the heyday of the ship or can be used to recreate her appearance with any certainty. One source is Michel Felice Cornè's large series of original gouaches illustrating the ship during her most active years. Many of his works were painted not too long after her victories or on commission from one of the ship's officers. However, Cornè also painted copies of his own work that were sent around the United States to celebrate the ship's victories that often differed in several details. The reasons for the discrepancies include having to quickly paint copies for exhibitions and working from memory.

A second contemporary resource is the model made by *Constitution*'s crew for Isaac Hull after their defeat of *Guerrier* in 1812. As a 'sailor model' made by eye, this is not to be taken as a scale model in the usual sense and some of the hull proportions do not accord with Humphreys' draught. However, it is valuable because it shows details of what men who sailed on her would remember. For example, although the stern decoration may be out of proportion, it does provide a sense of what the decoration was like, and perhaps what the colours used to decorate the area were. It must also be remembered that the model has been cleaned and restored over the years with some details lost or altered as a result.

A third useful resource is a set of drawings of the *United States* drawn in 1818 by Charles Ware. *United States* was built under the supervision of Humphreys himself. The deck drawings, sail and rigging plans are particularly useful to the modeller. Additionally, a sheer plan of *President* taken off after her capture and taken into the Royal Navy would provide accurate hull lines. Supplementing these references is Donald Canney's *Sailing Warships of the US Navy* (2001) and Tyrone Martin's (1997/2003) *A Most Fortunate Ship* that provide a detailed accounting of the ship's appearance taken directly from *Constitution*'s logs, letters and diaries. For modelmakers, changes to the ship throughout her long career, particularly her rigging, are summarised in Martin's (2003) *Constitution Close Up: Minutiae for the Modeler and Artist*.

APPEARANCE AT LAUNCH AND COMMISSIONING TO 1803

As built, *Constitution* was a flush-decked with the quarterdeck enclosed by bulwarks. A single strip of planking formed the upper sills for the spar deck gunports. The forecastle and waist were enclosed by hammock nettings held in cranes that extended aft to the side entry port. Her draught measured at 23ft aft and 21ft 6in forward. Her head was constructed with only tail and foot rails with no weather bulwarks, gratings, or heads. No anchor ports, billboards or bridle ports were included. In June 1798, her armament was listed as 30 x 24-pounder long guns; 16 x 18-pounder long guns; and 14 x 12-pounder long guns. Guns and iron work were black. Gun carriages could be black, red, brown, or green as all were common colours. The American naval establishment had no formal painting regulations at this time.

A single pair of slightly curved wooden boat davits extended from the mizzen channels on each side of the ship, and a pair of straight davits extended aft through the transom below the cap rail. A single lantern of unknown pattern was fitted to the centre of the taffrail. The hull was coppered as high as the light water mark with sheet copper measuring 14in x 40in held in place with 40 copper nails per sheet. The quarterdeck bulwarks were pierced for seven guns a side and for fifteen guns at gun deck level. The berth decks were pierced with air-ports. Some of these air-ports cut through the main wale.

The hull was painted black above the gun deck streak, and below it *payed* (varnished) in a mixture of pitch and tar. The gun deck streak was an unknown shade of yellow ochre that began at the catheads and ended at the quarter galleries. The bottom edge of the streak was defined by the top of the main wale, and top edge by the upper sill of the gun deck ports. The forward end of the streak was half-round in shape. The outer face of the gunport lids was ochre and the inner face whitewashed. It is not clear if the ship had full gunport lids or half ports with hinged upper lids. Martin (2003) notes that the ship's log does not reference gunport half-lids until August 1803 which could mean that they were added in 1803 or were there all the time. It is also unclear if the gunport lids had hinges but may have been boards and/or bunting placed into the gunport around the gun to keep the weather out.

As built, the catheads were plain but in 1802 decorative cat faces were added to their ends. There are no precise illustrations of the figurehead but described as a Herculean figure with his left hand atop fasces and his right extending a scroll with a baton lying beneath him. It is not known if the figure was painted in bright colours, but paintings of the ship by Cornè in 1803 shows it in white. The same painting also depicted the decorative trailboards carrying simple vine and leaf mouldings that were not picked out in a contrasting colour such as white, but instead painted over in black. At the ship's launch, these mouldings could have been white, and simply painted over in service. Interestingly, the painting also shows an ochre pin stripe over the spar deck level sills that runs the length of the hull but no specific mention of it has been found aside from this one painting.

The Secretary of War, James McHenry, proposed that the sterns of all six original frigates '... should be all alike to shew they belong to one family and represented by an Eagle in the Center with the Constellations around him, supported on each Quarter by the figures of Liberty and Justice' (from Martin, 2003). Commodore Edward Preble who was in command in 1804 commissioned Cornè to show his ship off the shores of Tripoli in 1804. This painting showed a spread eagle uppermost and centred on the transom above crossed cannon and cannon balls; two quarter figures representing Liberty and Justice, and two flanking Nereids in reclining positions who in turn were flanked by pairs of cannon, one cannon resting atop the other on either side of the eagle; and an assortment of stars, garlands, and rope 'framing' around and between the six stern windows separated by pilasters. The quarter galleries were also decorated with vine and leaf mouldings. Unlike the head decorations, all the stern and quarterdeck decorations are shown picked out in white – although some of the Cornè paintings show them all in ochre, but his paintings consistently show the windowsills and frames in red.

There are no known records of mast and spar finishing. The Cornè painting shows the inner and outer third of the bowsprit black or brown, with middle third, together with jib and flying jib booms in yellow ochre. For the masts, lower, top, and topgallant sections are yellow ochre to the trucks with blackened caps. The fore and main mast bands are blackened, with no bands depicted on the mizzen. Yards are black or varnished wood. A spritsail yard was originally in place at commissioning but was removed by Captain Nicholson by the end of 1802. Paintings show the fighting tops in clear finished wood. With regards to the dimensions of the masts and yards, in January 1796 the naval constructors were told they were at liberty to determine the dimensions for their respective ships. Martin's 2003 *Close Up* provides several detailed tables that attempt to determine mast and yard dimensions based on logs and practices of the day.

Canney (2001) notes that the ship was difficult to sail due to her over-sparring, plus the heavy frames and ballast that caused her to plunge and roll. He notes that as launched she was fitted with a conventional rig, but typically carried sails only as high as the royals. On 14 July 1800, Captain Talbot ordered a new thicker mainmast that stood 101.5ft tall and thicker at the cap but was 4ft shorter than the original to better withstand the press of canvas carried.

The number of boats established is unknown, but by the end of 1802 it is known that several (up to eight) were carried, with one in the stern davits, and one on the port and starboard quarter davits with the remainder nested on chocks in the waist. The outer hulls were painted white (and likely the interiors as well) but it was not uncommon to repaint the hulls different colours to identify each at a distance. One of the cutters was reported to have been painted blue, and paintings show some of them in green. The interior colour of the boats is unknown but could be white or, as shown in some period illustrations, the colour of the hull.

APPEARANCE CHANGES IN 1804

Under Captain Preble, the ship's log on 22 February 1804 notes that the ship's gangways between the mainmast and foremast chains were planked up to provide new bulwarks to accommodate 6 x 24-pounder additional long guns borrowed from the King of the Two Sicilies for action against Tripoli. The six new guns were mounted in the quarterdeck gunports and the existing 12-pounder guns relocated to the new waist gunports. The total battery consisted of 36 x 24-pounder and 14 x 12-pounder long guns; 8 x 32-pounder carronades were carried but their location is unclear. Hanging shot lockers were added to both sides of the main and spar gun decks.

Billboards (properly *anchor palm blocks*) were known to be fitted under the first spar deck gunport by this time due to references made to their repair in May. On 12 September off Tripoli, *Constitution* collided with *President* destroying the figurehead and trailboards. In Malta the damage was rectified with a plain billet head and trailboards, and the area between the two uppermost head rails boarded up. The new head was described as very plain with very little, if any sculpture. The decorative rails that rounded the stern are listed as removed. The gratings and capstan are mentioned as being painted some unspecified colour.

APPEARANCE CHANGES 1807 TO 1809

In the summer of 1807 Captain Campbell transferred 4 x 32-pounder carronades to *Hornet* leaving *Constitution* with four carronades – two each on forecastle and quarterdeck with the long 12-pounder guns. On 18 July 1808, a new billet head, trailboards, quarter gallery and decorations were received. The decorations resemble those seen on the model built for Isaac Hull by his crew in 1812. The ship was rearmed with 30 of a new model (longer) 24-pounder

A view of the inner spar deck bulwarks showing the colour of the various fittings sported by the ship today. (*Evan Gale Collection*)

long gun from Cecil ironworks, plus 24 x 32-pounder carronades fitted to the spar deck. Guns were fitted with firing locks.

APPEARANCE CHANGES 1810 TO 1811

In August 1810 additional air-ports were cut into the hull along the berth deck on both sides up to the area below the catheads. By September 1810 the berth deck and steerage bulkheads were whitewashed, wales blackened, with the spar deck ceiling and one ship's boat's hull painted green. In December 1810 a new 'Charlie Noble' (stove smokestack) made and fitted, and a smokestack added to the wardroom stove. August 1811 the yellow ochre streak was painted white. The cutwater was also leaded.

1812 APPEARANCE

On 1 June, a trysail mast was fitted, and the spanker was rigged with sky poles to ease sail handling. A split dolphin striker was fitted to the bowsprit. Additional boats were taken on board: a third cutter, a 'green' boat, and gig were received on 9 June.

During the chase by the British squadron on 17 July 1812, Isaac Hull had the stern taffrail cut away to accommodate two stern chasers (one 18-pounder long gun moved from the forecastle and a larboard 24-pounder long gun taken from the gun deck). Two guns were also run out of stern cabin windows. In August the taffrail was repaired.

On 21 September bridle ports were cut into the hull mid-way between number one gunport and stem. These ports gave the ship the appearance of sixteen gunports on each side. In October 1812 the stern decoration received minor changes with the addition of five carvings resembling drops fitted between stern windows. William Bainbridge took command on 2 October 1812, and he had the gun deck raised by 5 inches between the fore and main masts to flatten the sheer and level the gun deck's surface to facilitate working the guns.

Olof Eriksen's book *All Sails up and Flying* identified some interesting aspects of the ship's rigging from the model built by Isaac Hull's crew. Gin blocks were used for the fore and main topsail yard ties, and that triple blocks on the fore and main channels were substituted for the forwardmost deadeyes that allowed the fore and main yards to be hauled around closer to the wind on sharp tacks.

APPEARANCE CHANGES IN 1813

On 11 February Bainbridge repainted the white streak to ochre to resemble British ships in an attempt at subterfuge. Captain Stewart took command on 18 July, and armament is now listed as 22 x 32-pounder carronades on the spar deck and 30 x 24-pounder long guns on the gun deck.

APPEARANCE CHANGES IN 1820

The ship underwent great repairs in 1820 with Isaac Hull back in command. Most notably, new Baker pumps replaced the chain pumps and spencers were fitted to fore and main masts. Spencers are gaff-headed fore and aft sails like a spanker but lacking the boom, intended to allow the ship to sail closer to the wind like a schooner. Sliding gunters were also fitted which could extend the height of the masts (probably to all three). A vertical spar was fixed to two iron hoops around the topmast that was raised and lowered by a halyard that passed through the truck (a wooden ball or disk at the top of a mast, with holes in it through which flag halyards are passed) at the very top of the mast. The gunters were handled from the fighting top. Hull believed that they could be raised so skysails could be employed without having to carry the more conventional fixed sky poles in place over 200ft above the water. However, on 2 May 1821, conventional skysail masts were fitted to the royals because the sliding gunters were not successful. A ringtail – a form of stunsail – was also fitted to the spanker. The ship's armament was listed as 30 x 24-pounder long guns on gun deck. The spar deck carried 16 lug-mounted 32-pounder carronades, 6 forward and 10 aft. Two 'shifting gunades' – a cross between a carronade and a long gun – were placed into the quarterdeck gunports but intended to be moved as required.

1828–1835 APPEARANCE

Placed in ordinary in 1828, preparations for return to active service began in 1833 with direction to preserve the original form and dimensions of the ship. Visible changes by February 1834 included metal bilge pumps on the gun deck, two chain pumps installed abaft the mainmast, and two Baker's pumps forward. Broad direction was given on the new stern decorations to include relief carved work of scrolls or wreaths to guide the painter to pick them out in white. The billet head and curve of the cutwater were to be restored to their original shape and the head area was to be protected by 'close woodwork as was recently done with the *United States*.' In following this direction, the curve of the knee was raised considerably higher in relation to the stem that put the trailboards on a level with the lower edge of the gunports. The location and dimensions of the gunports themselves were to be a uniform two feet above the gun deck. The bridle ports were moved forward ten inches and made to the same dimensions as the gunports.

When in command in March 1834, Captain Elliot commissioned a figurehead of then President Andrew Jackson in an attempt of to curry his favour, despite the 1815 regulations that limited the use of figureheads to ships of the line. Elliot also commissioned bas relief busts of Isaac Hull, William Bainbridge, and Charles Stewart and had them installed (presumably) on the stern of the ship. The figurehead enraged the citizens of Boston who were protesting Jackson's changes to the banking system, and the figurehead was decapitated at about the jaw line in protest. A tarpaulin later covered the vandalised figurehead.

On 26 October *Constitution*'s channels were moved to a higher position, situated so that their undersides would be placed on the lower part of the second strake above the spar deck sill. This placed the channel 16 to 17 inches higher than the spar deck and required that the channels be divided into a series of short platforms to be fitted between the spar deck gunports. The arrangements were heavily criticised and in 1835 blamed for nearly causing the loss of the ship. It is not known when the original channel arrangements were restored.

The ship sailed from Boston on 2 March 1835, with Captain Elliot in command. The gun streak was now painted white and carried all the way around the enclosed bow and cutwater. The defaced figurehead of Andrew Jackson was shrouded in canvas

A view of the guns on the restored museum ship. (*Evan Gale Collection*)

The deadeyes, channels, and chainplates carried by the ship today. The bulwark has been lowered to better represent the ship's 1812 appearance. (*Evan Gale Collection*)

painted with five red and white stripes. The figurehead was repaired on 14 March 1835 in New York, and iron plated billboards installed. Later in March, the ship sailed to the Mediterranean where Elliot and his officers collected livestock to take back to the US. The animals were penned *en masse* in the ship's waist beneath the boat skids. Included were five jackasses, one jenny, one Arabian bay horse, five Arabian mares, three Arabian colts, an Andalusian colt, three Andalusian hogs, and two Syrian hogs. To improve the pens, seven guns on either side of the ship had timbers fastened btween their trucks and the overhead beams to form animal stalls. The ship was derisively referred to as 'Elliot's Ark'.

APPEARANCE FROM 1842 TO 1852

The USN Board of Naval Commissioners decreed that ships' hulls were to be black with a white streak, and that inboard the bulwarks were to be either white, straw, or green. Polished brass was suitable for the cabin and wardroom quarterdeck rails only. *Constitution* joined the Home Squadron under Commodore Foxall Parker. In July 1842, 4 x 68-pounder Paixhans [shell] guns were in pairs in the midship ports on either side of the gun deck in place of the same number of 24-pounder guns. Despite the order, on 8 May 1844 the ship was repainted with white lead, and the gun streak red, but on 30 May 1845, the ship was repainted black with a white streak. In December 1846 the original Andrew Jackson figurehead was replaced with a new one. The new figurehead stood tall with a stern visage, clad in well-fitting attire topped by a draped cloak. It carried a scroll in his right hand and his left hand was tucked into the front of his tailed coat à la Napoléon. This figurehead may have been in full colour because it was noted as being repainted on the last days of the 1845–1846 cruise under Captain Percival.

When the ship was overhauled the chain pumps were replaced with suction pumps. New trailboards were carved like those seen on the ship today, but with a flower reminiscent of a Tudor Rose in the position currently occupied by the national shield. All her gunports were enlarged to be 3ft high and 42in across to accommodate new 32-pounder long guns and 8-inch Paixhan guns as main armament; 20 x 32-pounder long guns were located on the spar deck, while 26 x 32-pounders and four Paixians were located on the gun deck. There was a reversion to the older 1820 profile of the stem with the trailboards meeting the hull below the lower edge of the gunports. In 1847 the ship was observed to have the bulwarks extended completely around the spar deck only to be broken by 2ft 6in wide side entry ports. Hammock nettings extended from the catheads all the way to the taffrail. In 1852 Commodore Isaac Mayo took command. He erected new quarters on the spar deck abaft the mizzen mast consisting of a cabin that held a reception room, sleeping cabins for himself and his clerk, a clerk's office, pantry, and head. Windows were installed in the transom and in the two after gunports. On 28 October 1854, the log specifically referred to hinged half-lids for the gunports like those carried by the ship today.

1857 TRAINING SHIP

On 10 July 1857 the ship was converted into a school ship for the Naval Academy at Portsmouth Navy Yard. The waist was enclosed and bulwarks on forecastle and quarterdeck raised by planking-in the hammock stowage. The six stern transom lights were reduced to three, and the quarter galleries planked over with a single paned window cut centrally into the planks. The gun streak extended all the way to the after edge of the now-solid galleries.

US CENTENNIAL RESTORATION

In October 1871 a restoration of the ship was considered for the upcoming 1876 centennial celebrations. *Constitution* was to be repaired and restored as closely as possible to her original appearance. Work began in the spring of 1873 and during restoration decorative details of the ship changed. The figurehead was removed, and a new billet head carved and fitted. The rose on the trailboards was replaced with a national shield and the quarter galleries were fully glazed. The three bas reliefs were removed from the transom (although it is unclear if they were ever installed by Elliot), and the stern decoration was simplified, simply to emphasising an eagle and six stars like the ship carries today. Unfortunately, the restorations were incomplete for the centennial celebrations.

REDUCED IN RATE

Became a receiving ship with a housing built over her decks in late 1882.

1900s RESTORATION

A campaign to restore ship in Boston began in 1900, and by 1906 a superficial restoration of the ship was completed. The receiving ship deckhouse was removed, new masts, yards, and rigging were installed, and the upper and waist bulwarks lowered. A new billet head, with a dragon in the design (then thought to reproduce the 1812 style billet head) installed in place of the curlicue model of 1876. Stern decorations remained the same but were refurbished. Non-functional reproductions of 32-pounders were fitted to the spar deck along with batteries of 24-pounder long guns and 32-pounder carronades. Although they were far closer representations than the 1906–1907 guns they replaced, they still did not accurately reflect those guns carried in 1812.

By 1925 *Constitution* had once again fallen into a seriously decayed state, and in 1927 Lieutenant John Lord supervised a new restoration. His restoration significantly altered the ship's appearance. This work can be seen in photographs of the ship, and much of that work remains on the ship today. *Constitution* was recommissioned on 31 July 1931, and the ship toured the United States stopping in several Atlantic and Pacific ports.

MODERN RESTORATIONS

In preparation for the 1976 bicentennial celebrations, she was refurbished and repaired, but making no significant changes to her 1927 restoration. A subsequent refurbishment in 1992–1996 maintained her 1927 appearance until the 2007–2010 restoration that recreated aspects of her 1812 appearance, including lowering the bulwarks to just above the spar deck gunports and opening the waist bulwarks alongside the main hatch and replacing them with hammock cranes. She sailed unassisted for the first time in 116 years on 21 July 1997; it was also to be the last time. The ship is open for visitors at the *USS Constitution Museum* in Boston.

The ship as she rests in Boston Harbour today. (*Evan Gale Collection*)

62 USS CONSTITUTION: 44-gun frigate 1797

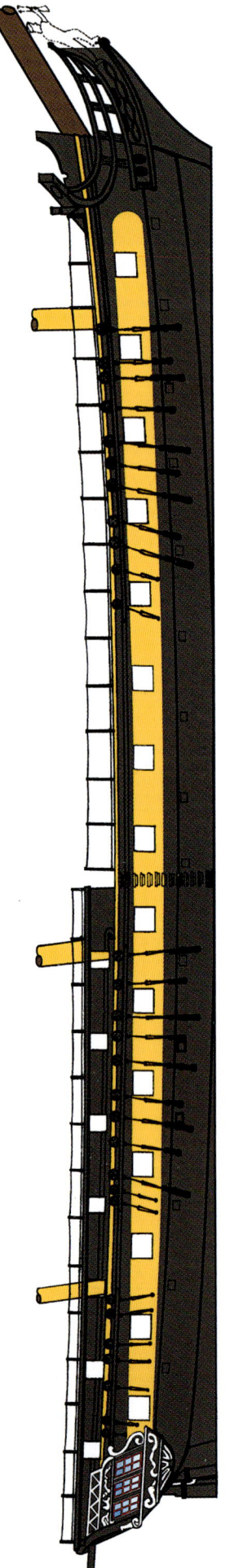

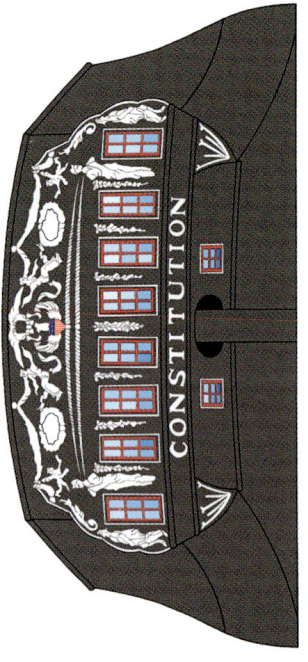

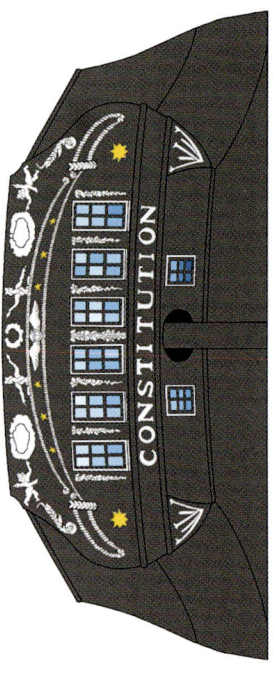

Constitution's 1803 appearance. This profile is based in the Humphreys draught (pages 2-3) and the colour scheme taken from Corne's painting shown on page 9. The quarter gallery decoration has been shown in white, although it may have been ochre as shown in at least one other depiction by this artist (for example, on page 8). Of interest is that the decorations of the head were not picked out in white but painted over in black.

Constitution's transom from 1803. The details of the transom were taken from written descriptions and examination of Corne's numerous paintings.

Constitution's 1812 appearance. This profile illustrates the notable modifications to the hull recorded in logs and other descriptions of the ship, such as the change to the forecastle bulwarks, the addition of a bridle port, and standing rigging changes that replaced deadeyes with triple blocks. The colour scheme was taken from the model built by Isaac Hull's crew in 1812 (pages 11-13). The quarter gallery roof has been shown in copper as per some paintings, but it may have been painted black as shown on the model. The model shows the underwater hull in green to represent the green patina of the ship's copper bottom after immersion in salt water.

Constitution's transom in late 1812. Illustrated is *Constitution's* transom after the damage from the encounter with *Guerriere* was repaired. The log records minor changes to the decoration as depicted. The stars and details are shown in gold but could just as well have been white. The transom during her escape from the British squadron and encounter with *Guerriere* earlier in the year is depicted by the Isaac Hull model.

COLOUR SCHEMES 63

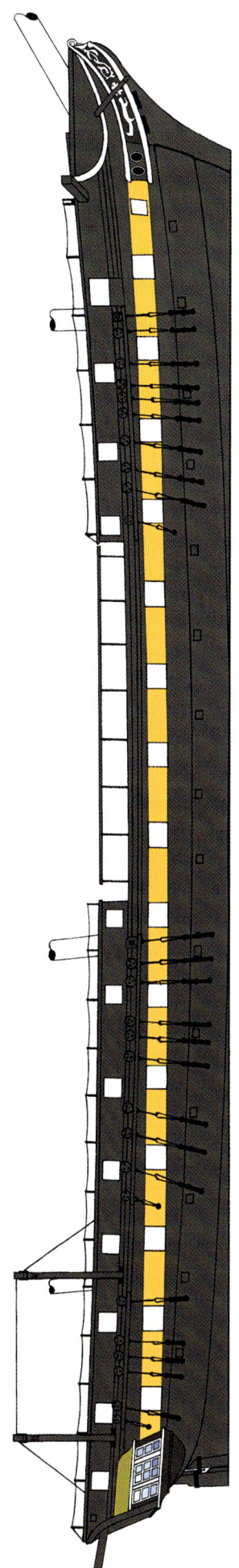

Constitution's 1815 appearance. The primary change noted at that Captain Stewart had the white stripe painted ochre. There are no other records of significant changes from her late 1812 appearance. The form and decoration of the transom was likely that carried in late 1812.

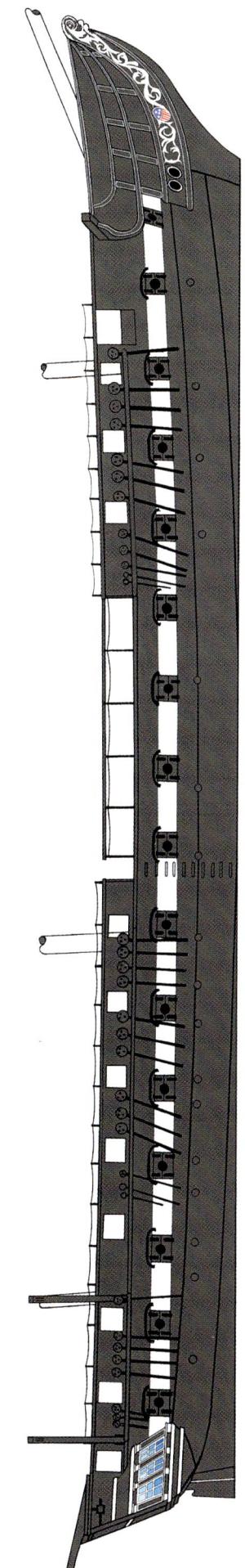

Constitution's appearance in 1976. The 1927 restoration significantly changed the ship's appearance, specifically the height of the bulwarks and profile of the stem and cheeks. For the 1976 Bicentennial celebrations the ship was not much different from 1927.

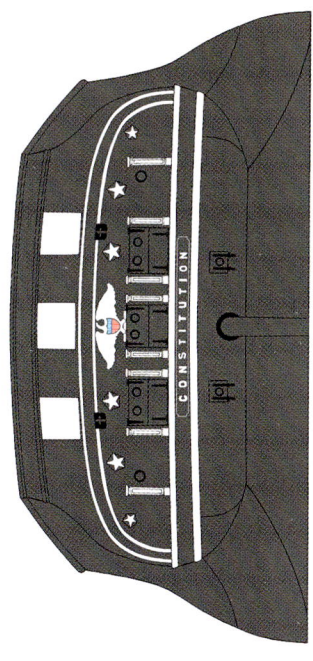

Constitution's transom in 1976. This style of stern was fitted in the 1870s and remained on the ship in 1976 and is carried today. The ship's name in 1976 was not painted directly on the transom but painted on a name board and fixed to the transom.

Selected References

BIBLIOGRAPHY

Boudriot, J, *The Seventy Four Gun Ship*, Vols I-IV (ANCRE, Paris 1986).

Canney, D L, *Sailing Warships of the US Navy* (Chatham Publishing, London 2001).

Dudley, W S, *Inside the US Navy of 1812–1815* (Johns Hopkins, Baltimore 2021).

Erikson, O A, *Constitution: All Sails Up and Flying* (Outskirts, Colorado 2009).

Gardiner, R, (ed), *The Naval War of 1812* (Chatham Publishing, London 1998).

Gardiner, R, *Frigates of the Napoleonic Wars* (Chatham Publishing, London 2006).

Goodwin, P, *The Construction and Fitting of the Sailing Man of War 1650–1850* (Conway Maritime Press, London & Naval Institute Press, Annapolis 1987).

Hezog, C, 'The Entwined History of Slavery and the US Navy' (2022). https://ussconstitutionmuseum.org/2022/11/30/the-entwined-history-of-slavery-and-the-u-s-navy/

Hoffman, R & Lyndow, K, *Structural Evaluation of Diagonal Riders for the USS Constitution* (Naval Surface Warfare Center, Bethesda 1993).

Jang, K L, *Ship Models from the Age of Sail: Building and enhancing commercial kits* (Seaforth Publishing, Barnsley 2022).

Jang, K L, *Sailing Ships from Plastic Kits.* (Seaforth Publishing, Barnsley 2024).

Lambert, A, *The Challenge. Britain against America in the Naval War of 1812* (Faber & Faber, London 2012).

Leyland, J, *The Royal Navy: Its Influence in English History and in the Growth of Empire* (Putnam, New York 1914).

Martin, T G, *A Most Fortunate Ship* (Naval Institute Press, Annapolis 1997).

Martin. T G, *Constitution close up: Minutiae for the modeler and artist* (no publisher, 2003).

Marquardt, K-H, *The 44-gun frigate USS Constitution* (Conway, London 2005).

RESEARCH

For both plastic and wood ship modeller an organisation dedicated to maritime research and modelmaking is the Nautical Research Guild (NRG), 237 South Lincoln Street, Westmont IL, 60559-1917585-968-8111. https://www.thenrg.org/. Membership of this organisation includes its journal that features articles on research, history, and plenty of modelmaking. The NRG hosts a huge website called Model Ship World https://modelshipworld.com/. This website has kit reviews and hundreds of build logs for model ships, including several of *Constitution* built in different materials.

ACKNOWLEDGEMENTS

Special thanks to Kate Monea, Manager of Curatorial Affairs, USS Constitution Museum, Boston, and Margherita M Desy, Historian, USN, Naval History & Heritage Command Detachment Boston for their invaluable assistance. Any and all errors in this work are the responsibility of the author.

KITS AND ACCESSORIES – WEBSITES

Bluejacket Shipcrafters	http://www.bluejacketinc.com/
Cornwall Model Boats	https://www.cornwallmodelboats.co.uk/
Dusek Ship Models	https://www.dusekshipkits.com/products/
Hannants	https://www.hannants.co.uk/
HiSModel	https://www.hismodel.com/
Langton Miniatures	http://www.rodlangton.com/napoleonic/list.htm
Model Monkey	https://www.model-monkey.com/
Model Expo	https://modelexpo-online.com/